INDIE AUTHOR CONFIDENTIAL 2

SECRETS NO ONE WILL TELL YOU ABOUT BEING A WRITER

M.L. RONN

ABOUT THIS SERIES

This isn't your typical writing self-help book. This series is a compilation of lessons learned from an indie author trying to walk the path to success. Follow author M.L. Ronn (Michael La Ronn) as he navigates what it means to master the craft of writing, marketing, and running a profitable publishing business. Learn from his successes and failures, and learn about things that most successful authors only talk about behind the scenes.

To read all the collected volumes of this series in an anthology, visit www.authorlevelup.com/confidential.

CONTENTS

BECOME A TECHNOLOGY-DRIVEN WRITER

BECOME A DATA-DRIVEN WRITER

BECOME THE WRITER OF THE FUTURE

IDEAS YOU CAN STEAL

INTRODUCTION

At the time of this writing, the COVID-19 pandemic continues, and I continue my commitment to learning how to level up my game as an author. I also continue my commitment to sharing my lessons learned with you.

Volume 1 of this series covers April through June 2020, which was around the start of the pandemic shutdowns. My learning was unfocused and wandering as I dealt with the early challenges of the shutdowns. My biggest goal was to ensure that my family and writing business would be in a position to weather the figurative storm. That quarter was tough to navigate because everyday life threw a curveball at me.

The easiest thing for me to focus on during the last volume was building my business's infrastructure. It was a great time to work on problems I had put off for a long time, like how to calculate my sales commissions accurately.

This volume (Volume 2) covers the third quarter of the year —July through September 2020. You'll find that my main focus throughout the quarter was still on infrastructure, but late in the quarter, I shifted toward production and writing again.

August through October of this year will be what I affectionately call "Beast Mode." Since I didn't write many books during the first half of the year, I'm aiming for a strong three months with a lot of books at the end of it. I'm going into beast mode so I can have a strong production year despite everything that's going on in the world.

In many ways, the lessons I learned in this volume were preparing me for "Beast Mode," but I didn't realize it until I wrote this introduction. I look forward to sharing the results of my beast mode with you in Volume 3. In the meantime, the infrastructure lessons this quarter were very productive and insightful for me.

My Core Strategic Priorities

As a refresher, my mission is to create content that entertains and/or educates my audience, preferably both. I do this by focusing on five strategic priorities:

1. Become a world-class content creator
2. Become a world-class marketer
3. Become a technology-driven writer
4. Become a data-driven writer
5. Become the writer of the future

I believe these five priorities are most important for me to have a long-term sustainable career.

What's in This Volume

In the last volume, I created a novel way to track my sales. This quarter, I found ways to visualize my sales data.

In the last volume, I also explored the idea of a personalized rules engine for AI-assisted editing of my manuscripts. I had a major breakthrough with that idea. Turns out it's much easier to accomplish than I thought. Shockingly easier.

I cover a lot of new ground too.

I experienced a three-day-long power outage that put my business contingency plan to the test. Because of good planning, I didn't lose momentum on my work-in-progress (though I did lose everything in my fridge). If you don't know what a business contingency plan is, you're in for a fun adventure!

I also made the biggest sales blunder of the year, costing me hundreds of dollars.

I hired a video editor, which was a major level up for my career.

I explored the ins and outs of browser-based writing apps, introducing my community to a new and competitive sector of the writing app space.

I continued my lessons in becoming a data-driven writer by finding new ways to think about my books as data points.

And, I came up with some pretty unique and interesting ideas for you to steal too.

There's plenty to explore, and hopefully, this book will inspire you to think about your writing business differently.

Thanks for reading this very experimental series. My sincerest hope is that it helps you in some way.

M.L. Ronn
Des Moines, Iowa
September 15, 2020

BECOME A WORLD-CLASS CONTENT CREATOR

MASCULINE VS. FEMININE
PROBLEM-SOLVING

I read a great book called *The Laws of Human Nature* by Robert Greene. It's a guide to understanding human nature so you can build your influence and impact. The book is a modern-day Machiavellian handbook, though I don't think Greene intended for this to be the case.

An early highlight in the book was when Greene explained the difference between feminine and masculine problem-solving. The term isn't meant to be sexist; there are men who use feminine problem-solving and vice versa. Understanding both styles is key to learning how to influence people because you need to change your style to suit others' preferences.

As a general statement, Greene wrote that females tend to have a non-confrontational approach to solving problems. They "feel" their way through problems and succeed by drawing on relationships with others to build consensus. This is the opposite of how males approach a problem, which is usually by throwing themselves into a problem and figuring a way out.

There's no right or wrong way, but it's helpful to know the style of the people you're trying to persuade. I found the advice to be particularly helpful in my job with corporate America this year, but I also think it's true of human nature in general.

What might your characters' problem-solving style look like? Wouldn't it be interesting to capture this little detail accurately on the page?

EDITING TABLE

I worked with a new editor for my book *150 Self-Publishing Questions Answered*, and she did something I've never seen before.

She added questions and comments in the manuscript about areas that didn't make sense, but then she pasted all of her editorial questions in a separate word document formatted as a table, with the comment, page number, and a column for me to respond if I wanted to.

This is an interesting idea because it keeps the manuscript uncluttered from unnecessary back and forth between the editor and me. More importantly, it's an important thing I can do for the editor up-front.

Instead of putting my questions as comments, I may create a separate Word document with my questions referenced there so the editor can answer them there instead of in the manuscript itself. It's an extra step, but it's cleaner.

EASY SOCIAL MEDIA VIDEOS

The website I use for stock images, audio, and video released a new service that allows you to create short videos using their stock content mixed with your own. It's a browser-based video editor, which is a novel idea that I've never seen before. Doubly smart is the ability to integrate it with their powerful content library.

In ten minutes, I had a great-looking social media video with images, audio, and video to promote one of my books.

I could have done this on my own, but the app made it more convenient. The app makes everything look more professional, which suits my goal of becoming a world-class content creator.

This was a pleasant surprise and another tool in my toolbox in the future.

HIRING A VIDEO EDITOR

I decided to hire a video editor for my YouTube channel this year. My schedule was so busy that it was the right time.

I've worked with a dedicated video editor in the past, so I knew what to expect.

My time is best spent strategizing, shooting videos, and connecting with my subscribers. Editing was eating up too much of my time each week, and the quality of my channel was suffering.

The first three videos were really about the editor and me getting to know each other. The videos weren't perfect, but they were much better than anything I could have done myself. Each video took approximately 7-10 hours to plan, shoot, and produce. Now that we're familiar with each other, it takes around 3-5 hours.

It takes me approximately two hours to plan a video, 30 minutes to shoot, 30 minutes to upload and communicate with the editor, and another 30 minutes to watch and provide feedback. That's around 4.5 hours, which, ironically, was about the time it took me to produce a video on my own.

While I didn't save a ton of time, I restructured my time so that it was more profitable. The time spent editing now goes to planning, which means that I can make more videos that will improve my subscriber count, views, and average view duration. I can now spend more time in the comments of my videos, assisting subscribers with their questions. I don't feel "rushed" to make videos like I used to.

By spending time doing the *right* activities, I'm happier and I make more money. It makes for a better experience for my subscribers too.

COURSEWORK

My first course took me almost two months to create. I had never created an online course before, and I wanted to take my time. I paid for it dearly because I stopped producing content for my YouTube channel for a few weeks.

My second course took about two weeks. I learned a lot from my first course, and I worked faster. I didn't get much sleep, but I created a premium course in a fraction of the time.

My third course also took about two weeks, but I improved the quality substantially and got more sleep. I did better planning because I knew what I needed to do and how many sessions it would take me. Even though it took two weeks, it was a leisurely two weeks.

My lesson learned is that you can indeed create a premium course in a short period of time. Courses are perhaps the biggest margin product you can create. Spend 20 hours to sell a course for $197. If your time is worth $50/hour, sell four units and you've just made a profit.

I once took a course where a guy sat on a couch in a hotel room for three hours and just talked about how to do something. He did the videos in one take with no editing. The course was very good, even though it wasn't highly produced. Ultimately, I just wanted the information. The production level didn't matter.

While I don't intend to turn my content into a course factory, I learned how to create a valuable course in record time when the time comes.

REDDIT

Lately, I've been following writing communities on Reddit. I use Reddit notifications as a way to generate ideas for new YouTube videos.

If I receive a notification about something, it's because people are talking about it. After I receive the notification and verify that it's on-brand for me, I review the post and look for the pain points.

For example, I saw a post on copyright. You'd think that people would have burning legal questions—but instead, so many wanted to know *how* to do the little copyright symbol on their keyboards. I made a series of copyright videos for authors, and I made sure to include the keyboard shortcuts in the video.

In many ways, Reddit is a streamlined way of doing market research. I'm starting to let Reddit notifications guide my content decisions, at least for the next quarter. Since I'm doubling down on my YouTube content, I need to make sure I'm in sync with what people talking about. I haven't always done a good job of that in the past.

YOUR BOOK AS A SERIES OF DATA POINTS

It took the indie community a long time to accept that a book is more than just a book; it's a product. In order to sell more books, thinking of them as products is useful.

I also believe that books are data. That data has immense power if we are willing to harness it. My sales database project in Vol. 1 of this series was a perfect example of harnessing the data around my books.

But what about my books themselves?

For marketing, this makes a lot of sense. Joanna Penn has said for a very long time that "the book is the metadata." Why should we have to choose silly keywords and categories when book retailers can scan our book and understand it on a deeper level? Amazon and Google are tech behemoths that have mastered the art of search—the keyword system is quite absurd if you really think about it.

At the time of this writing, YouTube engineers have admitted that YouTube's AI software can watch videos and understand them at a fifth-grade level. This means it can absorb the content of your video and make recommendations based on what it can understand. As such, tags are irrelevant there now.

It's just a matter of time before YouTube stops supporting them.

Amazon will follow a similar path eventually. Amazon has some of the best artificial intelligence engineers in the world. It's hard to imagine they don't have software that can read the millions of books on the Kindle platform and make decisions based on what it reads.

The very words we write are data. The purest example of this is a word count or statistics calculator in your writing app. It tells you how many words you wrote yesterday and today. That's data, and you can use that to make decisions. If you wrote 1,800 words Monday but only 500 on Tuesday, then you'll try to do better on Wednesday.

I've always believed that the text we create has unharnessed potential.

For example, in the first book in this series, I posed the idea of a "personalized rules engine," which is an app that can detect errors your editor caught in the past and warn you about them before you send your next book for editing. Once, I used the word "cadence" incorrectly in a sentence. I should have used interval instead. I use the word cadence all the time. Why waste my editor's time with an edit like that when I can fix it myself first?

Sometimes I accidentally leave articles out of sentences. My editor shouldn't have to fix mistakes like that.

This issue kept bothering me, so I decided to do something about it. Like I did with my sales database, I poured my time, money, and energy into solving this problem for myself, not knowing what would happen.

Turns out the solution was simple. I'll explain the technical details in the Technology section, but it involved using natural language processing (NLP), which is a subset of artificial intelligence. Long story short, I partnered with a developer to turn a test sample of editor recommendations *for Indie Author Confidential, Volume 1* into a series of if-then statements. The developer turned those statements into Python programming language commands. We used an open-source natural language processing (NLP) artificial intelligence model that was *free* on the Internet to process the commands into a Microsoft Word doc that had problem spots of the book marked as tracked changes.

Guess how long it took the programmer to do it?

Less than five hours.

In five hours, we harnessed the power of artificial intelligence to translate my words into data, and that data into real-life edits that Microsoft Word, Grammarly, and ProWritingAid couldn't catch.

As I build out my personal rules engine, I can now look at all of my books retroactively and turn many of my edits into code, and that code will alert me to potential mistakes, which will result in cleaner manuscripts and a better relationship with my editor so that she can focus on what really matters—my content and its meaning.

In many respects, if the project succeeds, my personal rules engine will be like a buffer between Grammarly and ProWritingAid and my editor, which is ironic because those apps are supposed to be a "last line of defense" before editing. Now they're the "second-to-last line of defense," I suppose.

A tool like this helps me on my journey to becoming a world-class content creator because it helps me deliver cleaner manuscripts that are more consistent from book to book. It's an invisible and subtle infrastructure change that will make a big difference over the life of my career, which ironically, is also the value proposition that artificial intelligence provides.

HOW TO DIE EMPTY

In a July 2020 guest interview, I received a question about how I remain creative after writing 50 books. The interviewer wanted to know if I've ever run out of ideas or if I struggled with writer's block.

I told her no, and then I gave an answer I've never talked about before.

In 2015, I read a book by Claudia Azula Altucher titled *Become an Idea Machine: Because Ideas are the Currency of the 21st Century.*

I love this book. I've read it several times. The main idea in the book is that coming up with new ideas is like exercising a muscle. The more you do it, the easier it gets. Altucher recommends coming up with ten ideas every day. It's tough at first, but becomes easier over time.

I've practiced that technique off and on over the years. The result is that I have digital idea notebooks with thousands of pages. The last one I checked was around 2,000 notes. That's just one notebook.

I have a notebook for fiction ideas (called my "sketchbook").

In fact, I used to read pages from my sketchbook on my *Writer's Journey* podcast every week for a year.

I have a notebook for business ideas and opportunities I want to pursue in the future.

I have a notebook for other random ideas that don't fit into the other two categories.

And, of course, I have this series, which is a collection of ideas. Every Friday, I receive an automated email reminder to write the weekly chapters of this book—one entry per strategic section with something I learned.

Some weeks, I didn't learn something new in a particular category, so I have to figure out what I'm going to say. I pull ideas out of the air almost every time. I have to think about all the content I consumed for the week and all the random ideas I had. I always ask, "What do authors need? What do I need in my business?" Then the idea comes almost every time. When it doesn't, I just wait a few hours. Usually, ideas come to me in floods, and I struggle to write them *all* down.

Oops, maybe I shouldn't have admitted that...But if you're reading this book, then you probably read the first book in this series, so your very presence here right now proves that my method works.

But, to be honest, I usually have more than one idea per category each week. As I write this, it's the end of July, and I already have around eight entries per category, which is more than double where I should be since each book is supposed to be 12 weeks long.

Anyway, the interview question made me critically examine my idea-generation process, and that's a good thing.

EMPATHY

This lesson is rambling and disjointed, but the topic is not an easy one, so bear with me.

I've struggled over the years with social skills. I've tried to work on improving them.

I wouldn't consider myself as someone who has high emotional intelligence. I care a great deal about people, but I've never been very good in social situations. It's just something I know about myself. It's one of those areas in life where I function, but not terribly well. When you talk to me, I listen more than I talk, mainly because I'm listening to understand. You can see "the wheels turning in my head." I struggle to process information in real-time, and by the time I have processed it, I have missed most of the social cues.

Instead, I tend to "feel" my way through social situations. I can't always read people very well, but I can read their emotions, and I rely on my intuition to help me determine whether I can trust someone or not. I call it social echolocation. Somehow I've managed to do pretty well for myself socially, even though I consider it a disability.

I do much better when I'm creating content. I can take my

time and craft my books to speak to people. I can put myself in other people's shoes much easier when I'm planning YouTube videos and podcasts too. The result is that no one would ever suspect that I'm socially awkward by watching my content.

It's one-way and one-sided, but in a weird way, my content builds so much trust that, when I meet with people, it's a lot easier for me to make connections. If I know which content resonated with them, then I know how to connect and help them on a deeper level. That builds more trust. In a way, I created a shortcut around my weakness and turned it into a strength.

I share this because I think a lot of writers are like me. We don't do terribly well in social situations, but we excel in the written word. It's not that we *lack* social skills; rather, we just have them in another format, and that format is not the common way that society expects them to manifest itself.

I reflected on this because, earlier this quarter, I was on a conference call with a writer who was asking me for some advice.

I've learned over the years not to ask about people's publishing situations. If someone tells me they have a publisher, I *never* ask who the publisher is. If it's a known, scammy publishing company, I have an ethical obligation to point that out to the author, namely because I am so open about self-publishing and I belong to a nonprofit that spends a significant amount of time exposing scammy publishing companies.

BUT...authors typically don't want to hear the fact that they're getting ripped off and their copyrights are getting stolen, even if it's true. The whole conversation just becomes awkward, and I lose the ability to help the author because they get defensive and shut down. I don't really lose much in the exchange other than my time, but I do like to help people if I can.

Like I said, I'm not going to ask about your publishing situation, but if you ask me my opinion, I'll tell you.

Anyway, I was speaking with this author, and we had a great conversation. A few weeks after our call, he emailed me and said his publisher wanted to charge him several hundred dollars for some publicity service that 100% of legitimate publishers do for free. The author asked me what I thought...

A basic Internet search confirmed my hunch that this was in fact a fraudulent situation. My ethical obligation kicked in, and I gave him the most diplomatic answer I could. I basically said, "That's not normal and not something you should pay for. You may wish to consider other ways to market your work without your publisher's assistance." I gave him enough to read between the lines, if he chose to do that. Then I walked away.

As I wrote the email, I tried to imagine myself in the writer's shoes—he probably didn't want to believe that he was living in a lie. He spent a year of his life writing a book, found someone who he thought believed in him and his work, and someone had finally validated him. He probably lived his whole life with the dream of becoming a writer, and he probably spent thousands of dollars already on this scam, possibly thousands he didn't have. In his mind, he was living in paradise, and who am I to tell him that the choices he made are going to come back to bite him later? Who am I to tell him that happiness isn't coming his way after all? If I were him, of course I would feel this way. From his perspective, he can't afford to lose.

You see, that's my problem. I knew all of this, but I said something anyway on the slim chance that maybe it would help him.

I never heard back from that writer, and I knew that would happen. It's not likely you'll ever hear about him either, because he and his book are screwed.

I've seen a lot of people come and go in the last eight years. The writers who leave the fastest are the ones who burn out, who never develop a thick skin, or those who are so embarrassed by unscrupulous people that they can't bear the thought of picking up the pen again.

I thought about this interaction quite a bit over the last few weeks. This guy had an amazing story, and he was very smart. His Achilles heel was that he was so *busy* that he wanted other people to do the work for him.

Writers' ability to place readers into the heads of characters and make readers laugh and cry along with those characters is, in my opinion, the ultimate empathy. In some ways, you could argue that writing is positive manipulation—it's the only kind readers sign up for. But writers also can't see when they are being manipulated. It's an interesting paradox.

There's a saying that scammers prey on the young, the old, and the stupid. Well, they also prey on the "very busy." This is why I constantly tell writers that you're never too busy to take control of your career. Busyness is an invitation for scammers to enter your life. This is why I am particularly careful, and it is also a reason why I have been extremely slow to outsource.

So, to conclude this long-winded chapter, my points are as follows.

If you don't have social skills, it's okay. Your skills and personal value lie in other areas, like writing.

If you have this problem, you will probably struggle to influence people, just like I did with that poor writer.

If you have this problem, you're also probably more vulnerable to scams than most people.

If you're too busy to wear the many different hats that are required in the self-publishing business, you're *especially* vulnerable to scams.

If you don't have social skills and you're too busy to take control of your career, you *will* get scammed. It's just a matter of time.

LESSONS FROM A THREE-DAY-LONG POWER OUTAGE

On August 10, a powerful derecho storm struck the state of Iowa. According to the Google dictionary, derechos are a line of intense, widespread, and fast-moving windstorms and sometimes thunderstorms that move across a great distance and are characterized by damaging winds.

The winds from the storm were approximately between 75 and 115 miles per hour, which is close to that of a category 3 hurricane. Derechos are called "inland hurricanes" for this reason. They are difficult to predict and seem to come out of nowhere.

Imagine my surprise as I was walking my dog and saw a giant gray wall of cumulonimbus clouds rapidly moving across my neighborhood. My dog was afraid—she wanted to go back home as soon as possible, and that never happens!

I gathered my wife and daughter and we hid in my basement until the storm passed. The lights blinked out Monday at 11AM, and we didn't have power again until Wednesday evening.

Do a web search for "Iowa derecho" and you'll see the destruction the storm ravaged on the state. It was unlike anything I've ever seen. There were trees down all over the neighborhood, taking power lines with them. Some trees fell on houses, sheds, and cars. Millions of acres of crops were destroyed, and this was already a bad year for farmers because of the COVID-19 pandemic. Three people died because they were caught in the storm unexpectedly.

The national media largely ignored the storm, but it was devastating to Iowans.

I was lucky. I only had a few tree limbs down in my yard, and I was able to easily pick them up. I also lost about two-hundred-dollars' worth of food in my refrigerator and freezer that spoiled. Other than that, we had to deal with a three-day-long power outage. There were some people in Iowa who didn't have power for weeks.

The outage came at the worst possible time. My phone was at 50%, my power bank was at 25%, and I hadn't yet recorded my content for the week.

However, I have a contingency plan for these types of situations. I keep a power bank to help me keep my phone charged because, during an outage like this, writing on my phone is the only kind of writing I can do.

I was in the middle of a new book, and I didn't want to lose momentum, so I used my phone to write. I could only write in small bursts at a time to save my battery. But I wrote about 300-1000 words each day, which is a win.

I also communicated with my audience that my content was going to be late for the week. I let people know on Twitter and YouTube. I believe it's important to communicate with your audience whenever you can't meet their expectations.

Fortunately, the power came back on and I was able to keep my streaks going without missing any content.

But the outage taught me some valuable lessons.

First, it tested my contingency plans. A contingency plan is a strategy of what you will do when disaster strikes. There are many different disasters that can strike a writer's career—damage to their home, the death of a relative, lawsuits, etc.

Anyway, writing on my phone is an easy way to get words in—since I do that every day, it kept me progressing on my novel. That was the first part of my contingency plan that worked well.

Second, my power bank has continued to prove itself a smart investment. I paid $50 for it on clearance, and it provided power for me when I didn't have access to an electrical outlet. This allowed me to devote 10% of my battery at a time to writing while keeping my phone available for emergency use.

Third, it confirmed my need to purchase a backup generator for my home. I plan to buy one sometime in the next year if I can. I don't need one to power my whole house—I just need it to power my phones, power banks, computers, and keep my fridge running for a few hours a day. I priced a solar-powered generator for about $500, which is useful because we can take it with us on family vacations as well.

Fourth, it allowed me to put my communication plan in action. When I took a YouTube hiatus in 2016, my biggest regret was that I failed to communicate with my audience about why I was leaving. I promised that I would never do that again. That plan largely worked, and my audience appreciated it.

Fifth, it's a great reminder of how life happens and how you often can't do anything about it. Even if I missed my YouTube or podcast content, I would have been fine with it because I communicated with my audience.

Sixth, I had some email successes and failures. I had about 20 emails in my inbox when the storm hit. When I received power back, I had about 100. That's a failure. However, I prioritized fan-mail, responding to fans even when I didn't have power. I even received and accepted two speaking engagements during the outage! My prioritization worked, but I didn't like how many emails I couldn't take action on. So many of the emails I received during the outage required me to be at my computer, which I don't like. I need to find ways to reduce my dependence on my laptop in responding to emails. If I could have remained inbox zero during the outage or close to it, I could have emerged from the ordeal with almost no real loss in productivity other than a lower daily word count. I'll need to think of ways to keep my emails low.

Anyway, I'm glad of where I ended up after the storm. It proves the importance of having contingency plans, particularly for power outages. Consistency is the key to being a successful author; being able to overcome little things like power outages can add up in a big way over the life of your career.

RECONNECTING WITH MY WHY

I wrote a book this quarter that was the most fun I'd had writing a book in years.

I did a YouTube video in early 2020 where I talked about how I created a "learning plan" for myself early in my career. I wrote down everything I didn't know much about, and I went off and learned it. I created deep, nested bullet lists for writing craft, business, marketing, technology, and more. And as I learned a new skill, I crossed it off the list. I made it a point of learning something new every day, and I improved my knowledge base substantially. My audience loved this idea and wanted to see me develop a learning plan for them.

My dilemma was that I didn't want to give people a book full of bullet points. That's boring.

I decided to take a risk. Instead of boring my readers to death, I wanted to convey the pathway to learning in a more instructive and creative way. So I wrote a book that mixes learning with storytelling and entertainment.

The book is called *The Indie Author Atlas: Your Guide to the Five Continents of the Writing World*. Essentially, I took the main bullet points that an author needs to learn and turned them into fictional places, then I wrote about them in the style of a Lonely Planet travel guide. It's a wacky idea, but it was so much fun to write. The book is the only one of its kind.

I mixed fiction storytelling style with my usual nonfiction writing style, which was unusual. Also, the book is written in the second-person POV, which is a first for me. The book contains custom illustrations that I commissioned.

All signs point to this book being either a winner or a complete dud—and that's exactly where I love to be as an artist. People will either "get it" or they'll say "that's the dumbest thing I've ever seen." I love that level of risk, and it's where I perform best, both in writing and business. This scares most authors.

You can trace an early prototype of this book back to my first novel, *Magic Souls: An Interactive Urban Fantasy*. It's a story about a woman who accidentally makes a deal with a demon and has to steal three souls to break the contract, or she'll lose her own soul. The story sounds dark, but it's actually not—it's quite sarcastic and ironic.

The reader controls the heroine, Bebe, as she navigates through various ethical train wrecks, because she has to manipulate and steal in order to save her own soul. One of the characters she has to manipulate is competing on a gameshow—and Bebe has to cheat her way onto the gameshow to get close to her mark. The gameshow is an actual gameshow—and the reader controls Bebe as she competes in various challenges. She can win or lose, and the story changes accordingly.

In the gameshow, the contestants can win different prizes—vacations, household appliances, and so on. Each prize had a short description inspired by television gameshows, accompanied by a public domain stock image.

Here's an example:

"BEBE WON A PARTY BUS PACKAGE!

"You and twenty friends will experience the city like never

before with a Megapimpin' Party Bus! Sure, this party bus looks like a school bus on the outside, but on the inside, it's a chic party room, retrofitted with comfortable seats, changing LED lights, a DJ, free premium alcohol, tinted windows for privacy, and a professional chauffeur who will take you anywhere you want to go. Climb aboard, and whatever you do, don't stop the pimpin'!"

And another:

"BEBE WON A PAIR OF CUSTOM BASKETBALL SHOES!

"Whether you love basketball or not, you'll love these shoes. B-Ball Shoes, Inc. has agreed to design a custom pair of shoes just for you! You'll visit the website and select your colors, soles, laces, bling, and other accessories that will make your shoes unlike anyone else's on the court. If you think your friends will be flabbergasted when they see your new kicks, wait until they see you dunk!"

These write-ups were inspired by hours and hours of watching gameshows as a kid.

Somehow, the memory of the gameshow in *Magic Souls* made its way back to me, and it inspired me to try writing in this style for an entire book.

Whether the book succeeds or not, I had a blast writing it. While writing it, I kept thinking, *This is what pure fun and entertainment feels like.* My hope is that readers will feel my joy when they're reading. If they don't, it's okay. I had an amazing two weeks writing the book, with really high word count days to be proud of.

I NEED A BETTER INTERNET
CONNECTION

Being a guest on *The Creative Penn* was one of the highlights of my author career when I appeared on the show in 2016. It accelerated my YouTube channel and increased my income substantially. I'll always be grateful to Joanna for that early momentum.

Imagine my surprise when she invited me to be on the show again in 2020 to promote my book *150 Self-Publishing Questions Answered*.

Joanna is a great interviewer because she reads your books and does a substantial amount of prep work prior to the interview. She also sends you the questions ahead of time, which just makes things easier for everyone. I spent a few days preparing for the show.

I joined the Zoom call and we chatted for a few minutes—everything was going smoothly. Then she started recording and we started the show. Out of nowhere, my Internet decided to stop working!

I had to do some quick thinking—this was only the biggest podcast interview that I did this year...

Luckily, I have an alternative Internet connection. I tried

that, and it didn't work! Thank God my neighbor let me use his Wi-Fi so we could complete the interview. Aside from being out of breath from racing to my neighbor's house, the interview went smoothly. You can definitely hear me out of breath, though. Bless Joanna for her patience and ability to edit the audio smoothly, so you won't even be able to tell that we had an interruption!

It was an incredibly embarrassing moment for me, especially because I pride myself on being professional, and I rarely have Internet issues.

After that moment, I swore that I would never let this happen again on a podcast interview. Ever.

I upgraded my Internet speed and hired an electrician to install ethernet ports in my home. This way, I can hardwire my computer to my ethernet instead of relying on Wi-Fi during a podcast interview. That should solve the problem. And the expense is tax-deductible!

Part of creating world-class content is not having Internet issues. This will improve my professionalism and make it easier for me to do livestreams in the future if I choose to do that.

BECOME A WORLD-CLASS MARKETER

DISTINGUISHING BETWEEN SALES AND SERVICE

I bought a car a few months ago. The salesman was fantastic. He worked with me to find a car that was right for my family, and he didn't try to force me into anything.

A few weeks after we bought the car, we received a threatening letter from our bank because they hadn't received the title yet.

I called the salesman, but he didn't return my calls. I had to call the company's corporate office to resolve the issue, which took longer than I liked.

I don't blame the salesman for what happened. I blame myself.

Salespeople are salespeople for a reason. They get paid to sell. That's when they're at their best. Force a salesperson into servicing the accounts they sell, and you will create one of the most miserable beings on the planet. It's not what they're born to do.

That's why every sales organization needs a servicing department. The proper way to draw the line between sales and service is to do a clean hand-off at the point of sale—let the customer know who they can call if they have a problem. Otherwise, they'll call the salesperson, which sets everyone up for failure.

Why is this important for writers?

Writers are salespeople. We do almost everything in the writing life with the goal of selling more books. Yet there are times when we must also wear a servicing hat. A great example is helping readers side-load books onto their reading devices. This is why Book Funnel became so popular; they created a servicing platform and took side-load servicing away from writers so they could focus on writing and selling more books.

As I scale, I think about the line between sales and service in my business often. I'm at my best when I'm writing, making YouTube videos and podcasts, communicating directly with readers, doing podcast interviews, and strategizing about the future. Yet I receive a fair amount of "how do I" and "where do I" emails from my contact form.

As much as possible, I try to answer common questions on my contact form page to eliminate as many of those questions as possible. I think of it as reader self-service.

In the future, I'll need to find ways to assign certain reader emails to an assistant. I love answering fan-mail, but it's probably not a good use of my time to answer questions like "do you have a video on outlining your novel?" or "which book of yours should I read first?" An assistant (or even an AI) can and should handle that for me so that I can spend my time with the more substantive fan emails. I'm not trying to diminish fan-mail—I love it. But you do have to be more efficient at some point.

KEY PERFORMANCE INDICATORS IN SALES

There's a famous saying about marketing that says that 50% of marketing is effective, but no one knows which 50%.

I know one thing that *is* effective: analyzing your data for trends. Every successful salesperson I've known has this trait, without exception.

I was fortunate enough to have the vice president of sales at a Fortune 100 company mentor me. He always asked about numbers. "It's how I'm built," he used to say. A tactic I learned from him was learning how to quantify (almost) everything you do. If you can't put numbers to what you're doing, you're in the dark. How will you know if a decision is the right one? Your gut is right nine times out of ten, but what about the one out of ten times?

After building my sales report database, I found myself in the pleasant but daunting position of sitting on a mountain of data but not knowing what to do with it. I could do anything I wanted, but I didn't know where to start.

I thought back to the conversations with my executive mentor, and that helped me determine a path.

First, I needed to determine my key performance indicators

(KPIs). A key performance indicator is a signal that shows whether the business is doing well or in trouble.

For my author business, I determined that my KPIs were as follows:

- Total revenue and net units sold
- Revenue and net units sold by book, series, and product lines such as my YouTube channel and online courses
- Percentage of revenue and net units sold from frontlist content and backlist content
- Year-over-year growth
- Profitability of each of my books, which is the amount I have earned to date on the book minus the cost to produce the book
- Revenue and net units sold by retailer
- Revenue and net units sold by country

There are so many other ways I can slice and dice my sales data, but I had to start somewhere.

VISUAL SALES DASHBOARD

I don't do well with raw data. I like spreadsheets, but I prefer to turn them into something useful. In my professional job, I work with a data science team that turns raw data into pretty visual dashboards.

I asked, "Why can't I do the same thing with my writing business?"

I used Microsoft Power BI to create a nice, simple dashboard that gives me access to all my key performance indicators at a moment's notice. It only took me about an hour. I can also export the data as PowerPoint so I have historical snapshots.

It's not enough to analyze the data. Because I'm not a data person by nature, I often forget data points or nuanced details as time goes by. I developed a log that I used to answer a couple of key questions:

- What is the data saying?
- Where are the outliers?
- Where am I strong?
- Where am I weak?
- What actions do I need to take today?

- What items do I need to follow-up on in my next review?

That helped me stay organized and get back into the "data mindset" in my monthly review.

The dashboard was a major success. The next step is to find a way to build a more comprehensive dashboard that includes items such as my YouTube analytics, website analytics, mailing list analytics, fan-mail analytics, and expenses. Imagine a one-stop shop where all your business data is visualized so you can make better decisions, with the ability to jump into Excel to do deeper analysis if you want. That's my goal.

PRE-VIDEO AD

A technique I used in the past to improve my sales was placing a video ad in front of my videos promoting my books.

In 2018, I created a Scrivener versus Ulysses Cage Match video comparing the pros and cons of each app. By chance, I happened to see a video on YouTube by a mega-YouTuber who inserted a video ad just before his videos that advertised a product he was selling. He used stock videos, hip-hop music, and he narrated over the top of it.

I decided to do that with my book *Be a Writing Machine*. I found stock footage of happy, smiling people reading and writing, and I cut them together in a 30-second ad. Then I narrated the ad to jazzy hip-hop music.

It was one of the smartest things I ever did—by luck, the Scrivener versus Ulysses video did very well, with over 36,000 views at the time of this writing. That's 36,000 people who see the ad for *Be a Writing Machine*, with hundreds more seeing it every week. That ad sells a ridiculous amount of books for me.

For my book *150 Self-Publishing Questions*, I tried to rekindle some of that old magic, but I wanted to be more intentional.

I picked videos that had a higher chance of being picked up by the YouTube algorithm. I produced algorithm-targeted videos for 8-10 weeks and put a new ad for *150 Self-Publishing Questions* in each video. Again, I used footage of happy people having fun and celebrating, with a link to the book at the end.

My reasoning is that while my audience might get tired of the ads after a while, if just one of those ten videos is successful, I will pretty much have guaranteed traffic and income for the book. The ad alone will make the book profitable. If more than one video is successful, well...then it's a jackpot.

I pay a yearly fee for stock media, so technically, it costs me nothing to create these ads. It took about 30 minutes of my time.

That's marketing I can believe in!

HTML EMAIL SIGNATURE

A friend of mine is a saleswoman. She has an attractive email signature with her headshot, contact information, and a call to action to schedule a call with her. She is good at her job and always has a steady stream of sales appointments.

Since my role at ALLi is a sales role, I decided to do the same thing.

I paid a freelancer on Fiverr to create an HTML email signature with my author headshot, contact information, and a clickable button to schedule a call with me that links to my calendar scheduling app where they can make an appointment.

It cost me $30.

I love this idea because it looks professional, and it creates a strong first impression.

EMAIL TIME SERVICE

Companies evaluate their employees by how quickly they respond to customer requests. The company I work for prides itself on the fact that a customer could speak to a live representative in about ten seconds on average.

I've tried to implement time service in my response to fan-mail. Generally, I try to respond to all fan-mail within 48 hours. Most times, it's sooner than that. Other times, I fail miserably.

When readers submit my contact form, I set expectations that I will respond in 24-48 hours. Then I do it.

It's great marketing when a reader sends me a note and I respond right away. It usually catches them off-guard, in the best possible way.

I recognize that this is tougher to do as you become more successful, but I've always believed that it pays to treat your fans right.

SALES IN ACTION

I stumbled upon a tweet about a new community app for influencers.

Instead of using Facebook Groups (which I loathe), Discord, or Reddit, this app allows you to create a community with similar functionality under your own label. Your fans sign up for accounts, and they can create threads, answer questions, and engage with you through a sleek interface that reminds me of a mixture between Slack and Facebook Groups.

A long time ago, I chose not to create a member community because I don't have the time or energy to maintain one. Also, I don't have the personality for it. But I recognize that it's a smart way to communicate with fans and keep them engaged. If and when I become a full-time author, implementing one will be the first thing on my to-do list.

I also like the idea of a fan community I can control. Given the volatility of so many social media sites lately, white label communities are worth paying for.

Anyway, I signed up to be on the waitlist for the service, mainly out of curiosity. I received an automated email from the founders who said that they'd personally be in touch with me in a few months to schedule a 20-minute demo.

I thought, *Wow. That's totally not scalable.*

But it's a great sales technique. They're meeting with everyone so they can learn sales objections. They want to hear every possible no and the reason behind it so they can defeat those objections in the future. I bet by the time they meet with me, they're going to be very smooth.

It reminded me of the lesson I learned in the book *New Sales Simplified* by Mike Weinberg. I discussed it in Vol. 1 of this series. In that book, Weinberg discusses a proven three-step sales method:

1. Choose a target
2. Employ weapons of attack
3. Develop a plan

It seems to me that the app's founders are still on step zero. They know who their prospective audience is, but they want to refine their targets. They're meeting with anyone under the sun who will listen to them so they can figure out who to go after in automated marketing campaigns on Facebook, Google, and YouTube. They're probably pitching *hard* at the end of their sales calls too.

We'll see if the technique works, but so far, there are some big names promoting their platform.

It's always fun to see sales techniques that I learned about previously in real life.

A DIFFERENT KIND OF BOOK
LAUNCH VIDEO

I saw a prominent YouTuber do something different with a product launch.

He announced that he had a new product out, and he talked about the basic product information, how well it was doing, how many people had bought it so far. Then he read a few reviews and put them on the screen.

He ended with a call to action that told people where to find the product as well as offered a special coupon code.

I liked that he was casual about it. It wasn't a "buy my product" launch video. Instead, it was, "I've got this new product, here's what people are saying about it, and here's where you can find it if you're interested."

It inspired me to try a similar video on my YouTube channel and podcasts with *150 Self-Publishing Questions Answered*.

TOTAL SALES FAILURE

I missed an easy sale this quarter that cost me at least one hundred dollars.

A reader reached out to me about buying one of my books. He wanted to buy copies of my books for his students to read as part of a virtual event.

He sent me a message on Facebook asking if he could buy my books from me.

I don't check Facebook that often, so I didn't see the message until three days after he sent it to me. I replied and told him yes. But I made a critical mistake that lost the sale, and I was angry at myself for it. Maybe you can learn from me.

Perhaps the best way to illustrate how I failed is to read the following transcript between me and my imaginary sales mentor...

Mentor: Tell me about that direct sales interaction.

Me: A reader reached out and asked to buy my books directly from me.

Mentor: Directly? Ebook or paperback? Audio?

Me: I don't know.

Mentor: You didn't find out?

Me: We didn't get that far.

Mentor: I noticed that you didn't reply to him for three days. That's unusual for you. What happened?

Me: He messaged me on Facebook, and I don't check it often.

Mentor: That's understandable, and I have two thoughts about that. First, when you replied the first time, why didn't you take the conversation to email?

Me: I wasn't thinking.

Mentor: Why didn't you ask for his email address, or give him yours?

Me: I did.

Mentor: Ah, you *did*, didn't you? But you didn't ask for it until six days after his original message. You replied to him after three days, and when he replied again, you forgot about Facebook again and didn't reply for three more days.

Me: Correct.

Mentor: Your lead went cold.

Me: That's a simple way to put it.

Mentor: My second thought was whether there is a way for you to prevent this in the future, such as an automated reply that directs readers to your email address.

Me: I'll look into it.

Mentor: So much in sales is about speed and ease of doing business. You failed in both of those areas.

Anyway, I committed a couple cardinal sins of sales, which is uncharacteristic of me. I've never done sales through social media like that before, so I wasn't comfortable in the venue, and it showed. As a result, I missed out on *at least* one hundred dollars in sales—a transaction that would have taken me just a few minutes to do. Literally, all I had to do was get the guy's address, send him a PayPal invoice, ship him the books directly from Amazon KDP Print, and send him a Book Funnel link to the ebook.

Automation would have been my friend here. A Facebook chatbot could have directed the reader to my email inbox or to a direct sales portal on my site. Turns out that Facebook allows you to do this with just a few clicks. Wow...very embarrassing to reveal my lack of knowledge of Facebook's new features!

I fixed this problem by creating an automated reply in Facebook that tells readers I don't check Facebook often. I give my personal email address for them to contact me.

Long term, I'll need to think about the best way to implement direct sales onto my Facebook pages directly. I know it's possible, as I used to have an integration with Selz.com where readers could buy my books from my Facebook page. That was several years ago, and the technology was clunky. I'm sure it's better now.

I learned from this experience, and I'll try to do better next time.

AN EPIC RANT ABOUT LAZINESS, SLIPSHOD CRAFTSMANSHIP, AND CLARITY, AND WHY CLARITY IS THE CURRENCY OF SUCCESSFUL PEOPLE

Someone told me that they didn't like all the responsibilities of being an author.

They didn't want to market. They didn't want to be a businessperson. They didn't want to think about the future. All they wanted to do was write. Yet they wanted to self-publish a book and have a successful self-publishing career.

If you meet me in person, I'm not ordinarily a jerk, but I had to be a jerk to this person, particularly because they were asking me to look at the "brilliant" book they had created. The book wasn't brilliant, and this person had no sense of reality.

So I was brutally honest with them. The cover was awful, the editing was practically non-existent, and the story needed work (from what little of it I read in the first chapter). I told them in no uncertain terms that if they wanted to be a successful self-publisher, that they would have to quit complaining and learn how to take control of their career.

They were mortified.

"But why is my cover bad?" they asked.

I replied with a question: "What instructions did you give your cover designer?"

They told me what I suspected—they didn't give their designer any meaningful instruction about the genre of their book, the true target audience, or the correct symbolism.

Then I asked, "In ten seconds, tell me who the target audience of your book is."

They also told me exactly what I suspected they would say —everyone.

And then I asked, "So you don't know what a book cover in your genre should look like. You don't know who the target audience is. And you're asking me why the book is not successful?"

And then I gave them what I hope was helpful advice. I told them, "If you don't want to wear all the hats that are required to be a self-published writer, that's fine. But it means you're going to have to pay people to wear some of those hats for you. And if you don't understand how to give clarity to the people you hire, then you're toast."

Furthermore, the author wasted *my* time because they weren't *clear* in what they wanted from *me*.

Anyway, I'll stop being a jerk now.

So much in marketing is about providing clarity. Clarity to your cover designer, clarity to your target audience, clarity to your readers about what you want them to do when they're finished reading. If you can't provide clarity, you're screwed.

Clarity is about putting yourself in the other person's shoes and trying to anticipate their thoughts.

When you decide to be a self-published writer, you may not know it, but you're signing up to be a leader. That means you're in charge of your career, everything is your responsibility, and *the work of everyone you hire* is your responsibility. When they do a bad job, it's not a reflection on them—it's a reflection on you. And if *you* have chosen to abdicate all your responsibility because you don't want to wear all the hats that are required, don't waste other people's time complaining when you only have yourself to blame.

Everyone's situation is different. I recognize that as an influencer, I have to have some empathy. We all have certain limitations, especially when it comes to children, aging parents, illnesses, and more. I don't minimize that, because it's a big deal. But writing is the only profession in the world where people bring unrealistic expectations onto the first day of the job.

In the working world, if a company offered you a job, but the hours were nights and weekends, but you couldn't work nights and weekends because of family obligations, you wouldn't take the job.

Yet when some people become writers, they understand the job description, yet they don't want to adhere to it.

Kristine Kathryn Rusch published a blog post this quarter that I appreciated because the gist of it is so powerful. In sum, she says that we're living through a pandemic—one of the worst social and economic disasters in our lifetimes—and writers are complaining about the work they have to do. This profession is *nothing* compared to what grocery store workers, first responders, and medical professionals have to deal with every day during this crisis. They risk their lives, and we sit in a chair and make stuff up, probably in our pajamas.

I hope this chapter gives you some clarity about what's really important, and why it's important to have radical clarity about why you signed up for this job.

REPEATING YOURSELF ON
PODCAST INTERVIEWS

I was on a podcast interview that was broadcast live. We were talking about one of my books. At the beginning of the show, I gave the name of the book as well as a link to find it on my website. I also gave the name and link at the end of the show.

However, there were people who joined the broadcast late. Those people kept asking for the link in the comments.

I learned that, on live shows, you can never say the name of your book and give the link too much—there's always going to be someone who misses it. But only saying it once or twice means you'll miss out on potential sales.

PRESS KIT: PAYING DIVIDENDS
SINCE 2014

I've had a press page on my website for years, mainly to attract public speaking events and improve my professionalism. You can view it at *www.authorlevelup.com/press*

The page highlights my speaking engagements in the past and shows potential venue organizers what they can expect if they have me as a guest at their event.

I also host a press kit on the page—it contains author bios in differing lengths, author headshots, book covers and descriptions for some of my best books, and so on. I engineered the press kit to make podcast interviewers' lives easier so that they don't have to hunt down information about me.

Interviewers *always* ask for at least a bio and a headshot. Always. By giving them a press kit that has these items baked in, it streamlines the interview process. When podcast hosts book time on my calendar using my calendaring app, the confirmation email contains a link to the press kit. I don't even have to *send* it anymore. My platform automates it!

Earlier this year, I was invited to speak at the annual Writer's Digest Conference. The editor-in-chief found my videos on YouTube and reached out. After we finalized the speaking terms, I sent her a copy of my press kit, and she said she could tell I've done this a few times. That's a great compliment coming from someone who organizes one of the largest events for writers in the United States.

When I receive compliments on the kit, I know it's working. You'd be shocked how much time venue organizers burn chasing down little things like author bios and headshots. Having all of this in one place improves my professionalism and scores big points, which increases the likelihood of being asked to speak at events again. It also makes organizers more likely to recommend me to others in their network. It's one of the smartest, earliest sales tools I implemented in my business. I didn't do many things right early in my career, but this was one of them.

On several occasions this quarter, I received compliments and kudos from podcast hosts and event organizers for making their marketing easier. That makes me proud, and also makes me think of ways to take my kit to the next level.

BECOME A TECHNOLOGY-DRIVEN WRITER

AMP FOR EMAIL

I saw an interesting post on Twitter where someone was talking about a revolutionary email they received from Google promoting the newest version of their Pixel Buds.

The email allowed people to click on a color palette and change the appearance of a photo of the earbuds. They could even add Pixel Buds to a shopping cart and purchase *directly from the email*. Read that last sentence again. People were shocked and curious how this could be done.

I found a copy of the email and everything people said was true. The email was marketing brilliance.

Turns out that the email was coded with Google AMP4Email.

Google's AMP is a web protocol that helps developers make pages optimized for mobile e-commerce. It uses dynamic content such as sliders, checkboxes, forms, and mobile-friendly designs and images. I didn't realize it was also for email. This explains why email marketing services allow you to upload HTML for your emails...

I then discovered that there are websites that dissect and analyze AMP-created emails as a way to help developers create beautiful, effective emails. One such website is www.really-goodemails.com.

Discovering this was like stumbling into a brand new world. This functionality redefines author email marketing. What if you sent out a dynamic email for your book launch instead of the same old text email? The only downside is that the new AMP4Email standard only works for about half of mobile users, but this number will increase over time.

As I think about the next iteration of my website, I plan to keep AMP4Email in mind so that I can synchronize the design between my site and my emails. Ultimately, once I adopt direct sales, it would be pretty cool to sell books directly from an email so that users never have to leave the email.

BE OPERATING SYSTEM-AGNOSTIC

I wonder how much time people of the world collectively spend arguing which operating system is better.

Windows, Mac OS, and Linux...

Instead of joining the conversation on which one you think is better, why not become platform-agnostic?

This year, I bought a new laptop and installed virtual machines on it. I have Windows, Mac OS, and Linux operating systems on the same machine. I'm used to Mac and Windows, but Linux is an interesting adventure for me.

Sometimes you need a tool that doesn't exist in your operating system. You can either settle for a subpar equivalent or do nothing. Personally, I'm tired of that.

I'm tired of owning a Mac and accepting gigantic trade-offs. Sure, Macs help me be more productive and I don't have to worry about viruses, but they're junk for data analysis and business intelligence. Windows computers can do much more and have more applications that can assist with more tasks, but Windows computers aren't built to last—they never truly were. Windows also has some odd quirks that I'm not a fan of.

Owning all three operating systems means that you can use

any tool you want. If you need a tool, just switch operating systems with the click of a button. It's like switching languages, like English to Spanish. Once you become fluent in another language, you don't think too hard about switching. You just do it.

Many people will probably resist this idea, and I understand that. It's not for everyone.

I'm simply just suggesting that the writer of the future needs every tool they can get—just as you don't want to be locked into exclusivity with Amazon's KDP Select, you shouldn't be locked into an operating system.

WRITING WITH GPT-3

On her blog, Joanna Penn shared a website of a researcher who played around with GPT-3, which is rumored to be the most powerful language model AI in existence right now.

The website shared the researcher's explorations with the GPT-3 beta, which can create text that is so convincing that the average person would never know it was written by an AI. The website shows experiments in poetry, horoscopes written in the style of Weird Al, Tom Swifties, and more. The experiments are exceedingly long, but they all illustrate one thing: GPT-3 is good. Really good.

I saw someone on Twitter remark that playing with it is like seeing the future. It certainly feels that way.

One of the takeaways for me was the following observation: "The first limit is that it remains hobbled by the limited context window. GPT-3 has no form of memory or recurrence, so it cannot see anything outside its limited...[to] (roughly, 500–1000 words). This means it cannot hope to write anything of any serious length, because the beginning will soon vanish over the event horizon, and it also limits its ability to engage in few-shot learning, for the same reason: the prompt+generation will quickly exceed the window length."

Very interesting. So the model can create convincing text, but it can't think. Or, at least, it doesn't seem like it can. The memory limitations are also interesting, and leads someone as old as me to think about floppy disks and CD storage. Those didn't have much memory either, but now, the amount of storage on a mere flash drive dwarfs even the biggest floppy disk capacities exponentially.

Another curious takeaway for me was a reaction to the experiment on Twitter that I think sums up how most average people feel about words written by AIs.

I paraphrase: "I don't think people will care. I prefer well-written stories by humans. I have no connection with an AI so therefore they can never write anything that has real feeling. I don't believe that AI writing will ever be interesting."

Those sound like words that will be laughed at in about ten to twenty years when this type of technology is the norm.

What does GPT-3 mean for indie writers?

I see something obvious. If GPT-3 creates text indistinguishable from a human, imagine what text from GPT-5 or GPT-6 will look like. It's almost as if there will be a real book industry, and then an "AI layer" on top of it where many consumers live. People will cross between the layers without even thinking.

Here's an inevitable scenario that's bound to happen, most likely in the realm of poetry or short works first. A publisher, a news organization, tech company, or a successful author is going to run an experiment. They're going to publish a book, possibly under a sham pen name. The book is going to sell ridiculously well. Then the publisher or author will reveal that they didn't write the book; an AI did. Readers will feel shocked, betrayed, angry, and sad. The publisher or author will have made an important point, and book retailers will amend their terms of service to require authors to disclose if a book is written by an AI. They might even build AI systems to detect AI-written books. Ultimately, legislators will institute laws to require disclosure if even one word in a book is AI-assisted, much like influencers have to disclose if a link is an affiliate link today.

It's not hard to imagine a future where a publisher will use a powerful AI to scan all the books in its catalogue to create something unique. Imagine a publishing executive who says one day, "What if we created a poet persona who was one-third Billy Collins, one-third Emily Dickinson, and one-third Maya Angelou, with a focus on social justice?" The AI model would read everything the three poets have ever done, as well as the entire corpus of tweets from Twitter and Instagram on social justice issues of the last fifteen years.

The publisher could do this because they hold the rights to the poets' work. In fact, traditional publishers are in the best position to do this because they don't have to worry about rights clearance. Publishers usually take every right under the sun. I doubt any poet signing a publishing contract in the last fifty years could have foreseen this type of rights licensing situation. Therefore, the publisher probably holds AI rights by default.

What ensues would be a new genre: designer poetry, where publishers spin new poetry collections based on work already published. Imagine the marketing on a collaboration between a hot new poet and Billy Collins. The publisher could make it look as if the two poets wrote the poems together. The work would introduce new generations to Collins' work and also be a vehicle for discovery; he would receive a royalty for every book sold, without having to do anything.

A lot of poets (and authors) would reject this technology and even sue over it, prompting novel discussions about copyright and moral rights in the age of AI. Does an author have the right to quash an AI derivative work of their books because they don't want to be associated with the technology? What if the AI writes content in your voice that you find morally reprehensible, or that is inconsistent with your author brand?

This is doable in the near future with poetry. Some could argue it's doable TODAY. For long-form fiction, the horizon seems further out.

The idea of "designer" books opens up a gigantic can of worms, one I won't discuss here. But where there are copyright infringement issues, one can also see immense opportunity. The technology isn't all bad.

Take Nora Roberts. She has written many, many books totaling millions of words. What if she created a new pen name based on her prior works? The name could be Nora.AI. All those fans who wanted to see more adventures from their favorite couple might get spinoff novels written by an AI in Nora's style. The work might need editing, but most of the heavy lifting would be done by the AI.

To the people that are thinking "No one would ever read that," consider this: society said the same thing about ebooks. Society also rejected the first iterations of the automobile, smartphone, cloud apps such as Google Docs, Uber, and so much more. Twenty years ago, would *anyone* have thought that opening rooms in your house to random strangers on vacation would have been a good idea? Of course not, but AirBnB is immensely popular now.

I believe that the sentiment "people will never read works by AIs" will one day join statements like "no one will ever buy a phone without physical buttons" or "no one will accept rides from strangers using their personal cars as taxis." It's such a foreign paradigm shift for us, but it won't be for future generations and other cultures.

Imagine finding a writer that you absolutely love, and then

spinning that writer's work with another writer you love, creating a fun hybrid. Pay a small fee and you can create whatever fiction experience you want based on the two writers' works. You get entertainment and the writers (hopefully) get paid. You can even design the narrator of the audiobook, like a voice in the style of Morgan Freeman.

Your designer book becomes a fashion statement that you can share with the reading community, and that becomes a feedback loop for writers and publishers looking to create more content quickly using technology. Tastes will change so quickly that publishers will need AI to assist them in following trends.

This might even create a class of haves and have nots— writers who have big enough bodies of work to command an AI model (and therefore more opportunities) and authors who do not.

Anyway, this is very interesting technology that has the power to disrupt the way we consume content. It's hard not to see it having a big impact of some kind.

STREAMLINING, AUTOMATION, AND OUTSOURCING

Streamlining. Automation. Outsourcing.

These are the three most important words in the writer of the future's toolbox, and shockingly underrated and underappreciated today.

The biggest problem with the writing life as it exists right now is that it is highly manual.

You have to write your book. You have to edit it. You have to market it. You have to do just about everything. Tools exist to help lighten the burden, but even with those tools, I would estimate that the writing life is somewhere between 80-90% manual. **In order to remain competitive in tomorrow's world of publishing, whatever it may look like, I suggest that we'll need to be somewhere around 40-50% manual. That means that we'll need to figure out a way to streamline, automate, or outsource 40-50% of our work so that we remain focused on the activities that matter—writing, marketing, and connecting with readers.** Otherwise, it'll be too difficult for us to stay nimble because we'll drown in our own work.

Will the writer of the future be able to think a thought and then see a finished novel and an executed marketing plan? Probably not. But we should ask what we can do to make our jobs less manual.

Let me explain the importance of moving from manual to automated with a simple equation: Time equals money.

Let's tackle time first. You only have so much time in the day. If you're a full-time author, you have more time; if you're a part-time author, you have less. Regardless of how much time you have, it's a finite resource.

We can divide time into three different categories: productive time, unproductive time, and wasted time.

Productive time is anything that leads to profit. Profit means producing more books, book sales, or growing assets such as your mailing list, for example.

Unproductive time is anything that you shouldn't be doing but that you have to do. If you spend tons of time fixing formatting errors in Microsoft Word, that's unproductive time. You can't avoid it, and it *will* hopefully result in profit (in the form of a book you can sell), but it will take longer.

Wasted time is anything you shouldn't be doing that doesn't lead to profit. Providing customer service to help readers get ebooks onto their devices is not a profit-generating activity. Readers have already bought the book and you're just servicing them.

When looking at activities, we have four options.

1. We can continue to do the task with no changes.
2. We can streamline the task, making it possible to accomplish the desired outcome or a similar

outcome, but with less time and effort. Streamlining may also mean eliminating the task altogether.
3. We can automate the task, which means that all or parts of the task will be done by software.
4. We can outsource the task, which means we hire an assistant to accomplish it.

Most writers immediately jump to outsourcing. It's "glamorous" to have an assistant, but I believe that doing this can be an expensive if not fatal mistake. Outsourcing should be the last step, not the first.

Take the notorious example of calculating your sales each month. An author who publishes their books "wide" and on all book retail platforms will receive anywhere from five to ten sales reports each month, each in a different format. They may also receive affiliate income and income from miscellaneous sources such as PayPal and Patreon. It's hard for them to figure out how much money they made, and harder to discern trends in their sales data.

As authors start making more money, some may decide to hire a virtual assistant to help them.

When I did my sales reports manually, it took me four to five hours per month.

Let's say it takes five hours per month to do your sales reports. A good virtual assistant commands at least $40 an hour. That's $200 per month for five hours of work, or $2,400 per year. If that sounds expensive and you aren't making much money from your books, it is. But when you're making more money, you can spend money on these type of tasks. Twenty-four hundred dollars is more palatable to a more successful author, but...if you're a six-figure author and make $100,000 per year, the virtual assistant expense would represent 2.4% of your *gross* annual income on *data entry* that probably won't be 100% correct. Really?

Also consider that the price of virtual assistants will continue to rise. Sales report calculation is tedious work, and when done manually, leads to people cobbling together their own home-brew systems. If virtual assistants quit (and they will), you'll have to train new people, which means your systems will break over time, leading to more rework for you.

Here's how I handled it. I recognized that a virtual assistant has no business handling my sales data in its raw form. Instead, I asked if there was a way to automate my sales reports so that a computer could handle it, with me serving as a steward to make sure my data was handled correctly. No data entry.

I researched existing tools on the market, and in about three weeks, I found a novel way to chain Microsoft Excel macros, Microsoft Powershell, Microsoft Access, and Microsoft Power BI together so that I only had to spend approximately 30 minutes each month aggregating my sales reports. The software handles everything, and it's 100% accurate every time. With the click of a button, I can see how much money I'm making, my top-performing books, and a geographical map of where my book sales are happening.

It cost me approximately 100 hours to learn the ins and outs of the software and how to create the best system for me, which I recognize is more than most people would want to spend. I also had to learn basic coding. To put 100 hours into perspective, it takes me about 40 hours to write a novel, so my time was worth 2.5 novels.

Money-wise, it cost me $79 for virtual machine software, $139 for Windows, and $150 in consulting fees to hire a developer to help me with some difficult code. Overall, my hard cost was $368.

That $368 system saved 4.5 hours every single month,

increased the accuracy of my data entry, and gave me unfettered access to my sales data, which helped me make better informed decisions that drove more sales into my business. The system should last me at least a decade because I'm using everyday technology that is widely available and supported.

Sure, I had to sacrifice a few books to do it, when you consider that it was taking me 4-5 hours per month to aggregate my sales manually, I was wasting 1.5 books per year already.

Now, the next logical step in the process would be to outsource the task. I've already built a standardized system that is far easier to train an assistant to use instead of expecting them to do everything manually. If it takes me 30 minutes each month, it'll take an assistant around an hour, which is $40 per month, or $480 per year. That's 0.004% of a gross annual income of $100,000. Much, much better. Also, it's a better use of my assistant's time and I'll be more likely to retain them.

My lesson: don't outsource anything that you can't stream-line and automate first. You'll overpay, be less efficient, and spend more time on it than you intended. You can't automate everything, but when you learn about the existing tools out there, you'll be surprised at what you can do, and how cheap it is.

WHY CHINA IS SO MUCH BETTER
AT AI

It occurred to me while studying AI that I wasn't paying enough attention to China.

I read an article in WIRED by Kai-Fu Lee, who is an international expert in artificial intelligence. He also wrote a great book called *AI Superpowers: China, Silicon Valley, and the New World Order*.

My key takeaways from the article were that while the biggest AI discoveries are happening in the United States, the most practical implementations are happening in China. A number of factors make this possible, namely speed and execution. China has a huge population to test new software and technology on, and its population is eager to accept new ways of doing things.

Chinese entrepreneurs are relentless too, adopting a fail fast and often model. They ideate much faster than entrepreneurs in the United States and are willing to accept losses because they can use the knowledge to succeed in their next opportunity. I thought this was particularly insightful. There were other cultural factors that Lee discussed in the article, and I recommend that you read it.

In general, it got me thinking about authors and ideating. What would it be like to fail fast and often as an author, at a breakneck pace? What could you learn? What might self-publishing in China look like? If language were no longer an issue between cultures and both US and Chinese authors sold books across the borders of their respective countries, in what ways would Chinese authors approach book sales and discoverability? It's all intriguing to think about.

LATEX

While researching book formatting, I stumbled upon a document preparation system called LaTex (pronounced "lah-teck").

LaTeX is typically used for typesetting difficult scientific or technical documents, but it can be used for any kind of book.

LaTeX is similar to a programming language, but it handles mathematics, charts, graphs, bibliographies, and indexes more easily than ebook formatting apps. Wiley and Sons (a traditional publisher), for example, has been known to use LaTeX for some of their technical guides.

There are LaTeX marketplaces where you can find templates for certain types of books—journals, essays, scientific articles, resumes, curricula vitae, and paperback books. Browsing through the marketplaces, I couldn't help but think LaTeX would be a unique way to format a writing book, particularly one with a lot of figures and graphs. It would require the right content, of course. It would be foolish to use LaTeX for LaTeX's sake, but I now consider it a tool in my toolbox the next time I have an unusual book that needs special formatting.

THE POWER OF THE BROWSER

On my YouTube channel, I reviewed a browser-based writing app that allowed users to create outlines in their browser. It was easy-to-use and built using an unusual code engine. I published a *video highlighting the software*.

Over 1,100 subscribers watched the video in 48 hours. I thought that they would have some trepidations about a browser-based app.

They didn't. In fact, they welcomed it. The only user who expressed concerns used an antivirus program that cleared his browsing history every day, which would have erased any content he created in the app. That was an insightful comment.

I learned not to discount the power of browser-based writing apps. As long as it looks good on desktop and mobile, there is a segment of the community who will use it. Some people can only access the Internet through a mobile phone and may prefer to use a browser instead of a dedicated app.

EMAIL AUTOMATION AND FILTERING

During the second quarter of this year, my email inbox was out of control. I'm normally an inbox zero person, but once the coronavirus pandemic broke out, a pandemic also broke out in my inbox...

It got so bad, I was missing out on sales opportunities because companies were emailing me with special offers to sponsor my YouTube channel. It was an embarrassing few months for me, and I'm not proud of the amount of time it took to respond. I also took a dreadful amount of time to respond to fan-mail, which is unusual for me.

At work, I use Outlook, and I love the program's rule engine because it allows you to apply rules to emails immediately when they hit your inbox. You can eliminate emails from your inbox very easily by automation.

I realized that I should have been doing this with my writing emails—no idea why I never thought of it.

I used Gmail's filter feature to start assigning rules to emails that came into my inbox. Doing this, I eliminated approximately 20-30 regular monthly emails, which represents about 1% of the emails I get on a monthly basis, but every little bit helps.

For example, when I make a purchase, I don't need to see the receipt. I have Gmail tag the receipt email as an expense and put it in a dedicated folder; this way, I can simply review all of my receipts at the end of the month instead of having to address each one individually as it arrives in my inbox.

While I wished I could have automated more of my inbox, I can rest knowing that my emails are as automated as they can be. Now, scale is my biggest problem; I don't receive enough emails to hire someone to help me with them yet, but that's on the horizon.

Once I start receiving over 2,000 emails per month, it will probably be time to hire an assistant. That would be around 65-70 emails per day. I'm only halfway there right now.

In an ideal world, I would prefer not to spend much time in my email inbox unless it's for fan-mail, important business emails, or special items that need my attention. I make more money when I'm not chained to my inbox because I can create content. Email drives my day right now, for better or worse, and I'm committed to finding better ways to minimize it. I don't see a path to email freedom that doesn't involve hyper-automation and hiring an assistant, unfortunately.

When I hire that person, I won't have to waste their time with emails that they don't need to see, as my inbox will already be optimized. That makes me more efficient, saves me more money in the long run, and respects a future assistant's time and skills so that they can do their best work and hopefully enjoy doing it.

NATURAL LANGUAGE PROCESSING
AND WRITERS

I've been learning about natural language processing (NLP), which is a discipline in artificial intelligence. Let's see how well I can teach it...

You're reading text right now. Or you're listening to it if you bought the audiobook version of this book. A computer can't read or understand text; it can only understand code.

Computers do best when they can analyze structured data, which is data that has a consistent, standardized structure. The sales report you receive each month from various retailers is a good example of structured data; with only a few exceptions, the report format is exactly the same each month. A computer can take that and do things with it, such as compile a database.

However, when we talk, that's unstructured data. Everyone speaks differently, with a different speed, with a different accent, and so on. Everyone *writes* differently too. This is what we call natural language.

Natural language processing takes natural language and converts it into data that a computer can understand and then process.

The mobile assistant on your phone is perhaps the most

ubiquitous example of natural language processing that you use every day without thinking about it. It converts your speech into data in almost real-time in order to answer your requests. You've seen NLP at work in other places, such as dictating a novel through Dragon by Nuance, speaking to a chatbot on a website when you need technical support, in developmental editing AI apps like Fictionary, and even Grammarly. Grammarly in particular uses natural language processing paired with machine learning to learn at a bigger and faster scale by reading the words of users around the world.

Natural language processing is all around us, but it is lesser known to consumers because all the buzz right now is around machine learning, neural networks, and sentiment analysis.

I watched a *basic video on NLP* and thought it was interesting, but I didn't see any applications to my writing business. Then I stumbled on *another video* where a programmer was explaining a proof of concept he built that involved creating a rules engine with simple conditions. The user was able to add conditions through a nice interface, which affected the code on the backend. That got me thinking—gosh, wouldn't it be nice if I could do that with grammar rules?

Imagine an app where you could program a rule like, "If the article 'a' appears before a plural noun or noun phrase, then highlight the noun with a comment that says 'check subject-verb agreement.'" That little idea led to a hunch that felt very similar to the one I felt before I discovered how to build my book database.

It turns out that the rules engine that programmer built was possible, and that what I was trying to do *was* natural language processing—I just hadn't connected the dots.

That was when I had the breakthrough idea—what if you could mix natural language processing with a programming language to create the engine that I envisioned?

The idea of dabbling with artificial intelligence scared the *hell* out of me. As I started researching the idea, I felt my anxiety growing. I thought, maybe for once I had taken on more than I could handle. The discomfort was very similar to what it feels like when you write the novel you don't think you're ready for yet. I've learned to greet that feeling instead of running away because you never know what will happen. Some of the most important experiences in my life happened because I said yes to opportunities that were way outside of my skill level at the time. I'll write about this in the "Writer of the Future" section because it's important.

Anyway, the next day, I learned the basics of the Java and Python programming languages by watching a bunch of coding videos at 2x speed. I watched so many videos and read so much technical documentation that my head hurt. Yet, still, I had that hunch. It wouldn't leave me.

I kept thinking, *It's not worth it for me to learn a programming language to build an app.* Sure, I could do it, but it would be a massive undertaking, and I wasn't a data scientist, so even if I could program something, there was no way I could build an AI model.

And then I thought, *Have other people done this work? Surely there have to be open-source models out there.*

That was when everything clicked. I found the Natural Language Toolkit, a development kit considered by many to be the best entryway into natural language processing. Many Python developers use it. The NLTK contains a bank of virtually every word in the English language, and it can break any sentence into parts of speech. Take the sentence "I like a ice cream sandwiches." NLTK would break down the sentence and assign "part of speech tags" that look like this:

I_NN (noun)

like_ VBP (verb, present tense)

a_DET (article, or determiner)

ice cream_JJ (adjective)

sandwiches_NNS (noun, plural)

You can probably see the grammatical error in the sentence. Now that NLTK has broken the sentence down into parts of speech that the computer can understand, we can now use the Python programming language to create a rule that says:

- Given that a subject and verb must agree,
- if determiner "a" precedes any plural noun or noun phrase,
- then in Microsoft Word, highlight the noun phrase, create a comment with the text "Check subject-verb agreement and check determiner"

The end result would alert me to a potential typo in the manuscript. The actual rule is far more technical than that, so I've oversimplified it for clarity's sake.

Microsoft Word's spell-checker would catch this error, but what if I could potentially program errors that Word's spell-checker or Grammarly would NOT catch?

I posed the concept to my community and asked if anyone had Python expertise. A loyal subscriber who is a Python developer reached out and offered to help me build a prototype with four rules. It worked amazingly well. The developer taught me how to maintain the prototype, as well as some pointers on how to create additional rules. Now all I have to do is learn a narrow use of Python instead of the entire language, and I can pay someone to check it for me.

This allows me to implement the following workflow:

1. Write a book
2. Send it to my editor

3. Turn a certain percentage of my editor's edits into if-then statements
4. Turn those if-then statements into rules
5. Run my personalized rules engine to catch any edits my editor would have corrected
6. Send my editor an objectively cleaner manuscript

I should point out that not every edit my editor recommends can be converted. Also, no rule will catch 100% of errors.

But the great thing about the engine is that I can feed all of my backlist manuscripts through it. The engine would house all of my correctable mistakes from my last 50 books. There's no way I can remember every single edit an editor makes. Also, I've had different editors over the years, some better than others. Also, sometimes editors miss errors. The rule engine serves as a last line of defense.

It's impossible to quantify the number of errors in a book, but let's pretend we can for a moment. Imagine that your work-in-progress has 100 errors. Your editor normally catches 90. What if the engine could catch 10 of the errors your editor would normally have to correct? That would produce a manuscript that is 11% cleaner. In theory, it *should* save your editor time and effort, which means they will return the manuscript to you faster. It might even save you a small amount of money. It would also *possibly* allow the editor to find some of the other 10 errors they might have missed since it's easier to find errors in a cleaner manuscript.

Also, consider some additional uses.

You could use the engine to enforce your own style guide to ensure that your book's style is consistent from book to book. For example, you might choose to handle ordered lists a certain way that you want your readers to instantly recognize.

You could also use the engine to make the book transition to audio better. You could train it to capture words that are difficult for a narrator to pronounce such as "grasp." Or, if you use phrases like "if you're reading this," you could have the tool flag the phrase to remind you to remain format neutral. Ironically, this was an idea that I proposed in the first book of the *Indie Author Confidential* series.

Anyway, the lesson I learned was that when I follow my hunches, they lead me to interesting places. Because I followed my gut, dared to venture into scary territory, used my network, and kept asking questions, I created another game-changing tool that can help me in becoming a world-class content creator, a technology and data-driven writer. And all the prototype took was five hours and less than 100 lines of code. So much technology is around us, and it's free or very affordable. You just have to be willing to search for it.

CALENDARING APP

I have conference calls with people in the publishing industry on a weekly, if not daily basis. I spend a lot of time going back and forth trying to negotiate the best time to meet. A lot of people I meet with live in the United Kingdom and Australia, which further complicates the problem.

A friend of mine recommended an automatic calendar service. Instead of going back and forth to find a "good time," he sends a link to his calendar, and the other person finds a time on it, and the service automatically creates a calendar invite for both parties. The app takes care of availability issues, time zones, and conference call links.

I resisted this for a long time, but I finally broke down and bought one. Man, was it a game-changer! I should have done it sooner. When I bought the service, the number of calls I booked increased overnight because I didn't have to worry about technical issues.

This service is now an essential part of my toolbox. I tested it out with podcast interviews. A prospective podcast host emailed me asking to be on their show, and I sent them the special link.

Within minutes, they grabbed time on my calendar. The service I bought also allows me to control the conversation further—the form captures what the podcast host wants to talk about, and the confirmation email contains a link to my press kit.

Once the booking is complete, I just forward the confirmation as a quick thank you and tell the host I look forward to speaking with them.

That's the power of technology, and it only costs me $80 per year. The return on investment from my combined podcast appearances is worth well more than that.

SOME THOUGHTS ON AUDIOBOOK
PRODUCTION EFFICIENCY

On my birthday, August 13, I received an email from Audible that they had accepted my first personally-narrated audiobook, *150 Self-Publishing Questions Answered*, without any technical issues or recommendations. It was a technical victory for me.

Before I recorded the audiobook, I decided to take a gamble. I hired an engineer to create an "audio template" for me. He took a sample chapter from the book and mastered it to meet Audible's technical specifications. He then saved those specifications as a "template" in the audio editing app we both use, and sent the template to me. I then imported the template and used it for the rest of the chapters in the book. My hope was that the entire book would pass Audible's QA, and for an entire month, I wondered if my strategy would pay off. My gamble was that it would, and if that was true, then I essentially bypassed the need for mastering or hiring an audio engineer in the future because I could use the template for everything.

Audible approved the audio with no concerns. This means that I can now record an audiobook and edit it, and then master it and get it ready with the click of a button. Huge efficiency win for me.

Ideally, if I could get my process to the point where I record the audiobook, and then have someone else edit it, and then I can master and upload, that would be perfect, but it's not that easy.

For starters, when I record a section, I don't know if the recording is 100% perfect until I listen to it later. I may mispronounce a word, there may be an imperfection in the audio, or I might accidentally bump my booth when I speak. If any of these things happen, I have to rerecord the entire sentence. I often have to rerecord a batch of sentences from the previous session the next morning, which is inefficient in my opinion, but unavoidable at the moment.

The most efficient way for me to record an audiobook would be as follows:

- I record an audiobook with the cleanest takes possible, which takes approximately two times the full length of the audiobook.
- I pass the book to an "assistant," who edits out the breath sounds and extraneous noises, and then recommends which sentences to rerecord.
- I rerecord bad takes in one session, verify that no errors exist, and send the new audio back to the assistant.
- The assistant then applies the audio specification template and uploads the audio for my review.
- I then have to listen to the entire book to make sure the job was done correctly, which would take approximately two times the full length of the audiobook. Then I would upload it to audiobook retailers.

This is the cleanest and most efficient way that would save

me the most time. For a four-hour audiobook, it would take me approximately eight hours to record, around one to two hours of back-and-forth with the assistant so that I can answer their questions and provide direction, four hours to listen to the final product, with one to two hours' buffer to communicate corrections, and another four hours to export the audio files and prepare them for publication. Overall, my time spend per audiobook would be around 15 to 20 hours. Naturally, that number increases drastically as the audiobook length increases.

But in this case, the editing *alone* would take 20 hours if I did it myself, so this workflow would halve the amount of time it takes to produce a personally-narrated audiobook.

However, the method would cost money. I'd have to pay the assistant a rate per finished hour. The only way to keep expenses under control would be to pay less than $100 per finished hour or the project becomes far more difficult to make profitable quickly.

I would have paid a professional narrator *at least* one hundred and fifty dollars per finished hour for my nonfiction titles. That's $600 for a professionally-narrated title. My method would cost $400, which makes you ask what the point is narrating a book myself if, for $200 more, I can pay a professional narrator who will do a much better job. Of course, a book narrated by the author is a great selling point, but it has to make financial sense too!

This is an interesting economic problem that I didn't find a clear solution to at the time of this writing. Where I left it was that there is probably a "first magic number" for audio length, where, under, it makes sense for me to handle the project myself. There would be a "second magic number" where it makes sense for me to hire a narrator because it will require too much time to record. I don't know what the numbers are yet, but I'll continue to explore the issue as I create more audiobooks.

BEWARE WEB CONNECTIONS FOR
GATHERING YOUR SALES

I'm seeing a few data services for writers pop up that promise to connect with Amazon to download your sales data for the purposes of helping you figure out how much money you're making. It requires your Amazon login credentials.

Be careful.

The companies are not bad—they're providing a good service for a good reason.

Amazon KDP's Terms of Service state: "4.3 Account Security. You are solely responsible for safeguarding and maintaining the confidentiality of your account username and password and are responsible for all activities that occur under your account, whether or not you have authorized the activities. You may not permit any third party to use the Program through your account and will not use the account of any third party. You agree to immediately notify Amazon of any unauthorized use of your username, password, or account."

This means that if you provide your login and password to a third party, and the third party uses that to log in to Amazon, you've violated the terms of service. Some service providers have received approval from Amazon to do this legitimately. Those are the ones you should use.

I stumbled across a fairly new service that grabs your Amazon sales data and prepares it into nice charts and graphs for you. However, their terms of service were horrifying. I paraphrase:

"We are not responsible for any violation of any retailer's terms of service, even if that violation is made aware to us. We make your data available to you. If your account is canceled, you bear the risk."

Really? You're asking people to pay an annual subscription for your service with the understanding that they're bearing the risk for a *service you are providing*?

This line of reasoning is best described as follows: "We're just helping you make sense of your data. These are your books and you have the right to aggregate their data as you so choose." Philosophically, the argument is correct, or at least it should be. Legally and contractually, however, it's inaccurate. Reread Amazon's terms. Just because you create metadata doesn't give you the right to do whatever you want with it...inside Amazon's ecosystem.

Most people are never going to read the terms of service. I'll let you reread the contract language above and draw your own conclusions about what you would do.

I'm writing a book right now called *The Author Income Problem*, and in it, I explain that web connections to retailers to download your sales data is a dangerous game that you shouldn't play.

BECOME A DATA-DRIVEN WRITER

EMAIL STATISTICS

I found a service that reads your email inbox and then provides a metric dashboard with important key performance indicators.

Here are my metrics for June 2020:

- I received 713 legitimate email messages and 487 spam messages
- Forty percent of my emails are spam
- I sent 217 messages to 87 *different* people
- My average response time is approximately 1.5 days
- Tuesdays are my heaviest email days, with an average of 10-17 emails per hour between the hours of 11AM and 3PM

As I reflect on those numbers, I'm proud of a 1.5 day time service. Ironically, I discovered this metric after I wrote the chapter on email time service. I'm proud that I am meeting the service levels that I promise on my contact form. Of course there are outliers, but I think I can be forgiven even for a three-day service time if I'm really busy, as long as my reader gets an adequate response to their email.

My email flow is a problem. Two emails at 10AM, 17 at 11AM, 15 at 12PM, and so on is a problem. I can't stop the emails from coming in, so there's nothing I can do about that. However, as I think about scaling in the future, knowing when my emails are the craziest is helpful information. Once I've automated my inbox to the optimum level, I'll have to hire an assistant to help me with email at some point. Giving them set times to check my email inbox is smart. If my average peak email times are Tuesday between 11AM and 3PM, I might have the assistant check my inbox at 11:30, 12:30, and 2:30PM, and then once or twice again throughout the day. If we can hit service levels during peak times, then non-peak service levels will be easier to maintain.

The only data the report didn't give me is *what* emails I received during the peak times. I can easily find that information, but it's more digging and analyzing than I want to do at this point. But when I'm ready, it would be helpful to know what percentage of the peak emails are fan-mail, sales emails, emails from my inner circle, newsletters, and so on.

EMAIL PARSING

Over the years, I've flirted with QuickBooks for taxes. I don't like it, but I always find myself reconsidering it for one major feature: the ability to send emails to a dedicated email address and have the information from that email show up as an expense without you having to do anything. The feature is amazing.

It's called "email parsing." It's when a system breaks an email into a series of data points and passes them into a database so that you can use them for something else.

Let's say that I purchase editing services from an editor, who sends me a receipt. An email parser will take the receipt email and break it down into:

- Name of the editor
- Email address of the editor
- Date of the transaction
- Amount
- Service rendered

The parser would then download the data into either an

Excel spreadsheet or an Access database. In this example, I might have a spreadsheet of my annual expenses, so the parser would create an entry with the expense for my accountant. All I have to do is send the spreadsheet to my accountant at the end of the year. No data entry on my part.

QuickBooks has this down to a science, and it's why a lot of people choose them. It's too bad the rest of the program is unappealing to me.

I wanted to find out if there was a way I could do email parsing on my own.

There are software-as-a-service providers (SaaS) and downloadable applications that help you do this. After about an hour of market research, I decided they were a little too expensive for me right now. Fifty dollars per month is not worth spending on a handful of emails you need parsed. My biggest need right now is parsing receipt emails so I can cut down on my accounting each month. It would save me about 30-45 minutes per month, which is about six to nine hours per year, or about 15-20% of the time it takes to produce a book.

As I grow my writing business, email parsing has other benefits that *will* be worth paying for. Imagine parsing all the emails you receive from fans to assess trends or get content ideas; or parsing the dates and times of when you receive emails to determine the best time to dedicate to responding; or, linking parsing to machine learning or a chatbot to generate automated responses to questions you receive most often (with your approval, of course). Maybe for those types of inquiries, you have an "assistant," who is really just a bot that answers the easy questions so you can focus on the harder ones. That technology already exists and will become cheaper over time.

I'm not suggesting you abandon your readers to a bot; I *am* suggesting that some people email you with the same old questions over again without bothering to do basic research. Rather than deleting their emails (which many authors probably do), perhaps we should give those people a lower level of customer service compared to someone who asks you a truly thoughtful question. But the key is that they'll still receive an answer they can use.

Anyway, I enjoyed my time learning about email parsing. It's knowledge I can use to drive efficiency in the future.

TELLING STORIES WITH DATA

I took a free data science course. It was a basic course that introduced the principles of data science to everyday people.

The instructor emphasized the power of storytelling when it comes to explaining data. You can have the most powerful data in the world, but if you put people to sleep, then it's useless.

The instructor gave a simple equation to illustrate the point: Story x Analysis = Value.

He offered some tips on better storytelling with data analysis that honestly helped me more with writing this book than it did with data analysis.

The big takeaway was to avoid egocentrism, which means assuming that everyone knows something. For example, I can't assume that everyone reading this series understands the business and data terms I use, so I'm careful to give basic explanations any time I mention something that might be obvious to me but not so obvious to you. I'm still working on getting better at that.

His conclusion was to remember that clients know very little or nothing about data; that's why they hire data scientists.

Readers pick up books about wizards because they don't know anything about wizards, or they're intrigued.

Just as avoiding egocentrism is helpful with nonfiction, it's also helpful in creating more engaging characters because you can have characters explain things about their lives that are obvious to the character but not so much to the reader.

Funny how I learned this from a data science course. Some things are universal.

SIMPSON'S PARADOX

Have you ever wondered how data can say one thing at the macro level but say something different at the micro level?

For example, I write fiction and nonfiction. Overall, my fiction sales are down somewhat. In looking at the big picture, you'd think that my fiction is on the decline. However, if you look at just the fiction sales, a few of my fiction titles are doing quite well each month.

This is called Simpson's Paradox, and it's a well-known phenomenon in statistics. In the free data science course I took, the instructor explained the often-used example of college admissions in the University of California-Berkeley, where admission results at the macro level showed that men were more likely to be admitted, but department-level statistics showed that women were accepted at higher rates into certain programs than others. In some departments, the acceptance rate for women was equal to or slightly higher than men.

Learning about the paradox was useful when looking at my sales data. It's a reminder to dig into your data and never take it at face value because there could be contradictions.

AGGREGATING ALL MY SALES
REPORTS: LESSONS LEARNED

In aggregating all my sale reports into a database, I learned a lot about my book sales.

For example, I learned that 65% of my ebook sales come from the United States. That's probably a decent number compared to most authors since I am not exclusive to Amazon, but it's a long-term problem I'll need to address. I need to reduce my dependence on Amazon *and* ebooks.

I also learned that audio, for the first time ever, eclipsed my ebook sales. It is now my leading sales format. That validated my decision to jump into audiobooks. In fact, my foray into audio was right on time.

I learned that in Canada, the majority of my readers live in Ontario. Thanks, Kobo!

I learned that the Pareto Principle is real—about 20% of my books drive 80% of my income.

I learned that YouTube AdSense is a bright spot for me that continues to grow at a rate of about 10-15% on average per year.

I also learned how truly volatile affiliate income can be. Last year was my best year in affiliate sales ever; this year may be my worst ever. It's crazy how up-and-down affiliate income is. You can't rely on it.

I learned other little nuances that aren't worth explaining here because they would probably bore you.

The lesson is that your sales data will tell you a lot. You have to be willing to assemble the pieces and allow it to talk.

BULK UPLOADING

I discovered a book retailer that I do not sell books at: Streetlib. They reach a few retailers that my other ebook aggregators such as Smashwords, Draft2Digital, and PublishDrive do not.

I immediately thought, *I should get my books on StreetLib!*

And then I thought, *Wait. I have over 50 books.*

And then, *That would be a pain the neck, Michael.*

And then, *Do they have a bulk upload feature so I can upload multiple books at once?*

Sure enough, they do. They don't support ONIX, which is a metadata standard I discussed in the first book in this series (so read that if you have no idea what ONIX is), but they do support a spreadsheet that basically has the same fields as an ONIX submission. Populate the spreadsheet, upload your book files and covers in a certain order, and boom—StreetLib will publish all your books simultaneously. Imagine the joy of publishing 50 books this way!

I'm not exaggerating when I say that the issue of bulk upload keeps me awake at night. It's the single most important short-term problem all indies will have in the future.

I *cannot* afford to upload my books one-by-one to new

retailers anymore. I simply have too many books now. Individual uploading is time-consuming, expensive, and it leaves me prone to making simple mistakes with data entry, like mistyping a title or a price. Little things will always go wrong, no matter how diligent I am. Individual uploading is also inefficient and too expensive to pay a virtual assistant to do, not to mention a liability since that person has access to your retailer passwords and bank information, not to mention the power to wreak pure havoc if they don't know what they're doing.

I *need* automation that will help me with data entry. I would much rather populate fields with the one true incarnation of my data—my book database, where I house things like the titles, book descriptions, prices, and keywords for all of my books. I built my book database earlier in the year precisely to help me with this problem so I could have one place to house the correct information for my books so I could keep everything consistent.

With StreetLib, my first thought was that I could use my book database to populate *most* of the needed fields on their required spreadsheet, then manually fill in the ones I don't have stored, as the answers are likely to be the same for all of my books. I could use Excel's autofill feature to great effect here.

Unfortunately, unlike other retailers that offer bulk upload, StreetLib requires an ISBN for ebooks. I don't like that because I am not a proponent of ebook ISBNs. I believe they are an inefficient expense that grants almost no benefits in return.

In this case, I'd have to purchase ISBNs solely to get my books onto Streetlib, which does not justify the cost. I could also distribute to Ingram Spark, but only for new titles moving forward. It didn't feel right. If other new book retailers offer bulk upload but require ISBNs for ebooks, I'll reconsider, but for now, I'm not distributing to StreetLib any time soon.

But I did learn that ONIX metadata management software also allows you to export to Microsoft Excel. ONIX has many additional fields that are specific to the publishing industry, such as book type and watermarks. These fields are useless to indies, but you have to have an entry in the field. I noticed that some of the fields I didn't have in my book database that StreetLib required were part of the ONIX standard. In the future, when I'm ready to start bulk uploading, I can export the data I have in my book database into one spreadsheet and the data that I have in ONIX into another spreadsheet and then join them together in the order StreetLib requires.

This would reduce data entry and improve accuracy. It would also allow me to bulk upload with unparalleled speed and execution.

Imagine with me for a moment: a new book retailer with immense potential pops up tomorrow. Tomorrow night, I have all 50 of my books uploaded. The day after tomorrow, they're published. That should be the goal we all strive for. That's the very definition of nimble.

Overall, at the time of this writing, it will cost me about $100 for ONIX metadata management software, $575 for 100 ISBNs, and about 10-15 hours of my time to get everything set up (or, a few hundred to pay a consultant if I run into roadblocks). Then, moving forward, there would be no additional cost and the time spend would decrease drastically.

While I'm not ready to invest in this technology yet, I'm glad that I now have a plan on how to execute it. Sometimes, the plan is the most important thing.

THE DATA-DRIVEN EDITOR

I talk all the time about how being data-driven will be an increasingly important aspect of being a writer.

Until now, I had never considered the idea of a data-driven editor.

If you think about it, book editors have the same efficiency problems as writers. The more clients an editor takes on, the more money they make, but there's only so much time in the day. What if editors could use software to assist them in working faster and smarter? It's intriguing.

I happened upon a startup that uses natural language processing to assess your story's weaknesses. That's not terribly remarkable; there are at least a dozen companies that offer something similar in a slightly different flavor.

What made this particular company unique was that they marketed their software to editors too. That made me sit up and pay attention. If the software is good, that's a winning value add for the editor. It helps them work smarter and faster through a manuscript, and produce a better work product.

Of course, this does beg an interesting long-term question: if you have access to developmental editing software and it's good enough for your purposes, why hire a developmental editor?

Developmental editing will become commoditized. It'll be like your hometown insurance agent in the United States. Decades ago, people relied on their agent's expertise to insure their homes, autos, boats, and more. Now people are buying insurance off the Internet from insurance companies directly. Agents have to differentiate themselves with service and expertise, and they're fighting a losing battle.

I see a world, not very long from now, where authors buy AI software for developmental edits, and authors with more money pay for a developmental editor who provides expertise and service.

I also see a dynamic shift where new authors will buy software because it's cheaper, and more established authors will hire real editors, who will serve more as consultants at a higher cost, offering a blended mix of editing, market research, and data analysis, probably around a specialized genre. It's the only way developmental editors will survive. The role will become more holistic, encompassing several disciplines. That's my hunch.

Anyway, I think just as authors must master technology and data to be more successful, so must our service providers. Imagine book cover designers that use computer vision AI to help them design better covers, for example. It's a very exciting future to think about, especially as the cost of technology decreases and becomes more accessible to small businesses.

GRAMMARLY SECURITY FLAW

You can't go anywhere on the Internet without seeing a Grammarly ad. If you're an author, their marketing team will find you.

I like Grammarly. It's no substitute for an editor, but it *can* help you find additional errors that Microsoft Word's spellchecker can't, especially for fiction. In fact, *I published a video on my YouTube channel* where I stress-tested Grammarly's accuracy.

In 2018, a white hat hacker discovered a security flaw in Grammarly's browser edition. The hacker found that Grammarly was leaking every keystroke a user made in the browser, not just inside Grammarly. Bad guys could have stolen credit card information, private emails, and more. It was a major security flaw. (Note that it affected the browser edition only, not the desktop versions). Grammarly fixed the bug very quickly, and it doesn't appear that any accounts were breached. This is why white hat hackers exist—to help organizations find flaws before the black hat hackers do.

I didn't find out about the security flaw until now. It raised serious questions for me about the viability of cloud-based AI software and browser-based writing apps. These apps don't process your work locally on your computer; instead, they pass it to the cloud, where it gets processed along with the words of other users using the service. There are numerous advantages to doing this.

Sure, anything can be hacked, but...a bestselling writer would be foolish to use a browser-based extension to write their books that doesn't have a track record of security. I once watched a talk by John Grisham where he said he was terrified of hackers. He uses two computers; one that is connected to the Internet, and another that is not connected to the Internet that houses all his manuscripts. If someone of his stature were hacked, it would be catastrophic.

You don't have to be at John Grisham's level to be concerned about getting hacked. I believe it's a legitimate exposure any author faces.

In the articles that covered the Grammarly bug, one person commented that every programmer will face the day that their code is tested by hackers. For some, that day comes sooner than others. But when it does, everything is at stake. And customers and their data are the collateral.

Grammarly has a strong development team. I wonder how good development teams at startups of the future will be, especially with cloud-based services for writers, which will have fewer resources than other industries.

PUBLISHDRIVE ABACUS

I was encouraged this quarter to see PublishDrive announce additional functionality to its Abacus tool.

Abacus allows co-authors to see a visual split of their royalties. If I write a book with you, and I'm the publisher, I can upload your sales reports to Abacus and it'll tell me exactly how much I owe you. You can also log in and view how much money you're owed.

This quarter, PublishDrive announced support for Ingram-Spark, Draft2Digital, Kobo, Google, and Apple Books sales reports. This means that co-authors who are "wide" and not exclusive to Amazon can now avail of the service, which is great.

I'm not crazy about the pricing, but that's a personal preference and I understand that they've got to make money and recoup their costs.

I don't see why PublishDrive can't turn Abacus into a service for single authors. In other words, why wouldn't a single author be able to upload all their books and see instantly how much money they made? Charge an annual fee, and I predict that the service would take off. Knowing PublishDrive, it's probably in their plans. They've shown themselves to be shrewd innovators with data and technology.

AUDIOBOOK INDUSTRY DATA ON
PHYSICAL AUDIOBOOKS

Spotify announced this quarter that it is getting into the audiobook game by hiring several people to head up a new audiobook division.

I also found a Canadian study about audiobook listening habits. It said that 40% of listeners borrow audiobooks from a public library in both digital and physical formats.

Furthermore, the study said, "When we combine channels that have both physical and digital options, we find that Amazon (Audible and Amazon physical formats) tops the list with 51%, followed by the library at 48% offering physical and digital formats."

My head exploded when I read that. People still listen to physical audiobooks?

I wanted to know if this was just a Canada thing or if there was a similar trend in other countries.

I found a study from the Audiobook Publishers Association (APA) that painted a different picture. While I wasn't able to access the raw data to verify it, the study didn't say which markets it was based on. I have to assume it's the US.

The study indicates that in 2014, digital sales were 69%

(based on dollar amounts). In 2018, they were 91. Physical unit sales were 27 % in 2014, and 7.8 % in 2018. Other formats such as pre-loaded MP3 items, book and CD box sets were two percent in 2014 and 0.8 in 2018.

In any case, physical audiobook habits are declining (I presume in the US). Also, it's probably worth mentioning that the digital number is probably much higher than 91 percent due to the fact that most self-published books don't have ISBNs, so therefore they are probably not included in the study. It might be closer to 96 or 98 percent in my estimation. I don't know *anyone* in the United States who listens to physical audiobooks. My mom does check out pre-loaded MP3 cartridges from the library from time to time, but I always considered that an exception rather than a rule.

I can only imagine that digital listening has trended upward in the two years since the study. Unlike music, audiobooks cannot exist on vinyl records, so I believe that CD audiobooks will truly be extinct in about five to seven years...in the United States.

Both studies paint drastically different pictures of the US and Canada. It doesn't mean that either of the studies is wrong, though. If both studies are true and truly representative of the markets, the difference between the US and Canada is probably explained by Audible's near-monopoly of the US market. If Spotify enters the audiobook market, their international presence ensures that most major countries will also migrate to digital, mainly because Audible doesn't have much of a presence outside of the United States, UK, and Canada. The data above supports that listeners will adopt digital quickly.

The question I kept asking myself while researching was whether it made sense to explore producing CD versions of my audiobooks. If there are other countries like Canada, then perhaps it makes sense. However, the conundrum is that the only place I'd be able to sell CD audiobooks is Amazon, which probably defeats the purpose.

CDs strike me as awfully inconvenient to produce, and the format is fading away.

If physical audiobook sales are shrinking internationally, and continue to do so in light of the audiobook subscription market heating up, it would be a foolish move to create CD audiobooks. Very foolish. I decided not to pursue it, as it would be too time-consuming and expensive to do, and a financial loss for me if I got it wrong. As much as I want to reach new readers, this doesn't seem to be the way to do it.

BEAST MODE DATA

From August 1, 2020 to October 31, 2020, I decided to go into "beast mode."

In beast mode, I write a ridiculous amount of books in a short period of time. Because I didn't write as many books as I planned during the first half of the year due to the pandemic, I wanted to change that and ensure that I had a solid production year.

During the month of August alone, I wrote almost 100,000 words and three nonfiction books. That equates to around 3,200 words per day. For one week, I was writing 5,000 words per day without breaking a sweat. That's a record for me. One day, I wrote 10,000 words alone.

If I wrote 5,000 words per day for fiction (which is very, very rare), I would be brain-fried.

The experience was helpful data for me because it showed me what my new limits are. If I want to write a nonfiction book quickly, I can do it.

PROTECTING YOUR DATA

Someone wrote me desperate because they lost all their data. They didn't think their writing app could fail, but it did, and it took their precious manuscript along with it.

The encounter was a reminder for me to review my backup systems regularly, and I'm passing that reminder along to you. You can't make data-driven decisions or think about your books as data points if your data gets destroyed!

At a minimum, I recommend the following backup methods:

- Backup feature within your app. Most modern apps offer a feature that will auto-backup your work every few minutes. This isn't a bulletproof backup method, but you should still use it because it's free.
- Cloud backups. Dropbox, Google Drive, or iCloud allow you to sync your work across devices and save it in the cloud. The cloud also won't save you, but it's still worth using because if you don't sync other storage-intensive items such as music or movies,

your entire library will fit comfortably within the free plans of these apps.

- External hard drive. You can buy one for less than $100. Buy two. Back up your computer to the external hard drives nightly and disconnect the drives from your computer when not in use. I also use Apple's Time Machine feature if I need to go back in time to a certain version of a file.

- Portable USB hard drives. These are so cheap these days, it pays to own a handful of them. Back up your manuscripts on them, then keep them safe and separate. Keep one in the security deposit box of your bank, for example.

- Backup service. I use Backblaze. It backs up everything on my computer AND my external hard drives several times a day and stores them in the cloud, with the ability to see and access your backups over time. Backblaze is my final layer of defense. You can download your backups at any time, and they'll ship you a hard drive with all your data on it if you need it. Backblaze has saved me a number of times. There are other similar services to Backblaze, so do your homework on which service works best for you. If you like Backblaze, however, you can buy it at www.authorlevelup.-com/Backblaze (paid link).

Protect your data. If something happens and you lose everything, it can be devastating.

BECOME THE WRITER OF
THE FUTURE

VISUALIZING THE CRAFT OF WRITING

A question I've asked myself repeatedly over the last few years is how to visualize the craft of writing.

I've always believed that if you can visualize something, you can understand it.

Data analysts don't wade through raw spreadsheets unless they have to. They turn those spreadsheets into graphs and charts so that they can see what the data is saying.

Why do we as writers wade through words as a way to understand how to learn writing craft? The words are important, but is there another way to help us learn the craft?

I've experimented with numerous tactics over the last few years.

I wrote a lead magnet called *The Writing Craft Playbook*. I identify mega bestseller techniques and try to explain them with simple drawings. The book was received very well by my audience and doubled my mailing list.

I produced a series of videos on YouTube illustrating the IRAC method. IRAC stands for issue, rule, analysis, and conclusion. It's used in law schools to study cases and I amended the method for authors to study books. I used animated Power Point slides to convey the techniques I studied. That also worked, but I found that the videos were too long.

I'm mainly including this learning in the book as a way to challenge other people. Writing a book is not the only way to teach writing craft. We should start experimenting with other ways that help us to become masters of the craft.

USAGE-BASED WRITING APPS

Which team of writers are you on?

Team A *abhors* paying subscription fees for anything, let alone writing apps. These writers have a personal vendetta against anything with a subscription.

Team B supports subscription-based services but would like more for their money.

Why not join Team C, which is writers who ask for usage-based writing apps?

Is such a thing possible? It's hard to imagine writers being okay with an app that works much like the utility bills they pay at their homes.

In today's environment, I don't think so. But I do think cryptocurrencies could make it possible.

It really is the best of both worlds.

Developers need a steady stream of income to support their applications. If they charge a one-time fee, they'll eventually reach a saturation point, which means they have to keep upgrading the app and charging for new versions to make money. Subscriptions ease this burden by giving them more reliable income, but users are leery of subscriptions because incompetent developers in the past took people's money, only to give them stability updates.

What if you could pay based on how much you use your writing app? You pay based on writing hours, which is an approximation of when the app is open and actively being used.

If you only write one or two books per year, you'll pay less than someone who writes ten. Power users could opt to buy themselves out of usage rates by paying a multiple of the average fee.

What do you think?

I tend to be on Team D—the team that doesn't think this payment model will work any time soon. I think writers would resist it. But if economic, technological, and market forces change in the right direction, it's not hard to see how this could happen.

DOWN GOES THE EBOOK! UP GOES THE AUDIOBOOK!

The German-based publication Bookwire and The Digital Book Report produced a virtual conference this year called All About Audio. Jane Friedman covered the biggest insights in her biweekly newsletter "The Hotsheet."

The highlights were that the audio industry could be split into two industries: audio and podcasting. Both are growing at a rapid rate, fast enough that the audio industry is set to surpass the ebook industry by 2023. The report cited subscription services and binge listening as being on the rise. It also said that audio-first publications will become more prominent. It also indicated strong frontlist and backlist sales, with the majority of unit sales coming from frontlist titles and the majority of listening time coming from backlist titles.

Overall, a glowing report for audio and audiobook sales, which validated my decision to double down on audiobooks. By 2023, I'll have a significant amount of titles in audio, more than I do now.

I'M NOT A GURU. I'M A GGDP

One of my most important decisions when I decided to create nonfiction books was that I didn't want to be a "guru."

I had an embarrassing little streak for about a year or so where I held myself out as an "author business coach," but those days are long behind me.

I've always been wary of a perception in our community that self-publishing influencers aren't trying to help authors—they're making money off them.

In my experience in getting to know many influencers in our community, that's not true, but the perception exists because there are unscrupulous people who give everyone else a bad name.

Therefore, I've never held myself out as a guru. Gurus take your money and expect you to treat them like gods.

Instead, I've always said that I'm just a writer trying to figure everything out, and I share knowledge as I obtain it in hopes that it will help someone. Sure, I write books and try to build my authority in the space, but my authority will always be based on my experience, and my experience is uniquely my own, not a prescription for other people. If you want to study my path, cool—I'll give you plenty to study, much of it for free. When I do charge money, I'm reasonable.

I'm not a guru. I'm a GGDP—guy going down a path. That's it.

I've watched "gurus" in other industries rise and fall. I don't want that future. I prefer to be a working professional who keeps getting better with every project.

TERMS OF SERVICE ALERT

I received an email from Amazon with an invitation to add my podcasts to its upcoming Amazon Music and Audible podcasts program.

I always review terms of service prior to signing any agreement. This one had a red flag. Essentially, people believed the terms said that one must agree not to disparage Amazon or any of its products in order for Amazon to distribute the show. A lot of people were really upset about this, but that's not technically what the terms said. The terms said that the content must not contain advertisements or messaging that disparages Amazon.

The legal question is, what did Amazon mean by "messaging?"

In law, if something isn't defined in a contract, courts look to the word's everyday meaning. According to Merriam-Webster, message is defined as:

1: a communication in writing, in speech, or by signals
Please take this message for me to my friend.
2 : a messenger's mission
the girl will go on a message to the shop

— Cahir Healy

3 : an underlying theme or idea

the message is that it is time to change

— The Economist

According to Wordnik.com, message is defined as:

n. A usually short communication transmitted by words, signals, or other means from one person, station, or group to another.

n. The substance of such a communication; the point or points conveyed.

Dictionary.com states:

1: a communication containing some information, news, advice, request, or the like, sent by messenger, telephone, email, or other means.

2: an official communication, as from a chief executive to a legislative body:

The definition that all of these sources have in common is that a message is intended to be a short communication. Only in one sense is it defined in a way that could be construed as a podcast.

One must then ask: if Amazon intended to exclude shows that disparaged it, why didn't it explicitly do so? It could have said "no content is allowed that disparages Amazon or its products" or it could have instituted an approval process. It didn't do that.

This leads me to believe that Amazon is on the lookout for a very narrow type of problem—probably shows that are deathly critical of it, or one that is sponsored by a competitor, for example. That's not 100% certain, and they can of course enforce this clause however they deem necessary, but one must question the company's intent.

The invitation created a media firestorm for Amazon, so my

guess was that they would revise their contract language to clarify their intent. (They did shortly after I wrote this chapter, so I was right. More on that in a moment.)

The next thing I looked for was exclusivity. Fortunately, they didn't require exclusivity. All a podcast host has to do is cancel their distribution with two days' notice.

So I signed the agreement.

First, I read all terms before I sign any contract.

Second, I never sign anything that I can't abide by.

Third, I always try to put myself in the shoes of the other party. Amazon is going to make this service available on its Alexa devices; therefore, it follows that they don't want Alexa saying things that make Alexa look bad...it would be the equivalent of a Pepsi worker drinking Coke on the job.

Fourth, I rarely discuss Amazon anyway. I tend not to speak poorly of the provider of my biggest source of income. That's common sense.

Fifth, if I don't like it, I can stop distributing my podcasts to Amazon. If they don't like it, they can stop my podcast's distribution, but they can't stop the distribution of my books.

Are we kidding ourselves when we pretend to be outraged that Amazon can bring down the hammer on us for disparaging it? Amazon routinely cancels people from its platform for any reason anyway, often for things they didn't do. They take a "guilty until proven innocent approach" in all things they do. That's not criticism; it's truth.

So I didn't see a real problem at this time. That could always change, and if it does, I or they can opt out of the contract any time.

Shortly after I wrote this, Amazon removed the offending clause from the terms altogether, so I was right in my analysis.

With terms of service, there is always an element of risk.

You balance what you can afford to lose with the potential bene-fit, and the potential of getting in on Amazon's podcast launch makes a lot of sense with my audio strategy.

.

ONE COMMAND CENTER

The writer of the future needs a unified command center. Not a writing app, a formatting app, a spelling and grammar app, and the myriad other software we use.

My workflow today is as follows: I write my books in Scrivener, then export them to Microsoft Word so that my editor can edit using track changes. I review the editor's edits in Microsoft Word, run the manuscript through ProWritingAid, copy/paste the book back into Scrivener, then export to Vellum for formatting.

I despise the workflow, but it's the best we have right now.

It's unreasonable to expect one app to execute on the level of Scrivener, Microsoft Word, ProWritingAid, *and* Vellum, but it is reasonable to ask that the writing apps of the future work together seamlessly.

I'd like to write my novel in Scrivener and be able to send it to my editor, perhaps by granting the editor permission to edit my Scrivener file with tracked changes (if Scrivener ever supports that). Preferably, I should never have to leave my writing app for anything, even formatting.

The bestselling writing apps on the market are extremely

vulnerable for disruption. Writers just don't realize it because the writing app as we know it hasn't changed in forty years and we can't conceive of how it can possibly evolve.

If a new writing app functioned similar to how I describe the following narrative, it would render the current landscape of writing apps irrelevant. Let's call it Shapeshifter.

Shapeshifter is a writing app that offers an interchangeable interface that supports WYSIWIG (what you see is what you get) writing interface a la Microsoft Word, or a markdown experience like Ulysses. With one click, you can change its appearance and therefore its layout. It's two or three different writing apps in one. That's the app's headlining feature. It "shapeshifts" extremely well, molding itself to suit the writer instead of asking the writer to adapt to it.

The desktop version is available on Windows and Linux. Mac users were originally left out, but they quickly learned that they could run the app by installing Windows on their computers—a deliberate and intelligent choice on the developers' part that allowed them to seize the Windows market, which was ripe for a new, modern competitor. Given the benefits you're about to hear, Mac users will have no qualms about upgrading their computers to quickly abandon their current writing app. Ironically, the app is available on iOS, iPad OS, and Android, with good feature parity so that users can write on-the-go no matter their phone or tablet.

Shapeshifter is also available in the browser, with an optimized writing experience.

No matter where you are or what device you are using, Shapeshifter will shift to suit your preference.

If that were it, Shapeshifter would be remarkable. But here's what makes it the writing app of the future: out of the box, the app itself is not terribly robust. It has a few key features such as a word processor and the ability to import and export.

However, the app has way more features available; you purchase what you need. If you don't need a distraction-free mode, you don't have to pay for it. If you ever want it, you pay a one-time fee of $5. The app and its features are like LEGOs that you can snap together based on your preferences. Every writer's app will look different; in fact, writers are encouraged to share their "space," which is linked to a generous affiliate program that rewards them for every referral they make.

Shapeshifter is also the first writing app other than Microsoft Word to offer third-party developer integration. The app's in-house features are comparable to most other writing apps, and without any integrations, it looks rather vanilla. Third-party integrations are where the app shines. Developers can create new kinds of writing tools—outlining features, dictation support, macros, and integration with other apps, like voice assistants. All of these plugins help you become a better version of yourself. This also allows the app to stay at the forefront of advancements in operating systems.

Shapeshifter offers a Discord or a Reddit community where users can request new plugins and developers can create them. The app gathers a cult following that quickly becomes mainstream.

Now, let's talk about the biggest selling point: the price.

Shapeshifter's developers wanted to create an affordable writing app and avoid the ire of the community by switching pricing models. For a one-time fee of $30, you pay to own the app. The developers keep the prices low because you pay a la carte for additional features such as cloud syncing between mobile and desktop and WordPress blog integration, for example. You only pay for the features you'll actually use. Overall, you might pay around $200-300 over the lifetime of the app, more including plugins, which can range from a couple dollars to a few hundred dollars depending on the plugin.

And that's not all...

Shapeshifter is just one app in a suite of apps for writers. Shapeshifter Writer handles the writing. You see, the developers figured out that it's impossible to do everything well in one app, so they modeled their app suite after the Adobe Creative Cloud so that all their apps work together seamlessly.

Shapeshifter Writer is an app and marketplace for *writing*.

When it's time to edit, the writer can, with the click of a button, "shift" the app into Editor mode, which is technically a separate application in its own right that you can also purchase.

Editor is optimized for editing. Shapeshifter Editor is a pioneering editing app that is designed solely for back-and-forth between a writer and editor. Drawing inspiration from apps like Google Docs and Asana, a writer and editor can collaborate on a manuscript without the manuscript ever leaving the Editor ecosystem. All the author has to do is invite the editor to join a given project. The editor can edit the book in a browser and does not need to purchase the software, though doing so under an Editor's license will grant them unique benefits.

All edits that the author accepts in Editor get pushed to Writer so that the manuscript is in sync everywhere. The author can of course revert and rollback changes at any time.

Editor also supports third-party integration, such as Grammarly, ProWritingAid, and anything else a developer can dream of in the editing process. Editor would also encourage and support artificial intelligence plugins.

When it's time to format your manuscript, you can "shift" to Shapeshifter Formatter with the click of a button. With just one click and a smooth wizard, you can have a publish-ready ebook and print edition. It offers the power of Vellum but also third-party integration for formatting templates and special features such as indexes. You could even grant access to a formatter who could upload HTML that the app would accept. Changes you make in Formatter are automatically synced with Writer and Editor.

Formatter even integrates with book retailer APIs so you can publish without having to leave the app.

Shapeshifter's holy triumvirate of Writer, Editor, and Formatter succeeds because it streamlines the process of writing and helps writers do more in less time. It takes advantage of the fact that some writing apps go years without receiving updates as well as writers' frustration with subscription-based apps. It leverages the power of Adobe-smooth integration between the three apps, with the ease of use and customization of Reaper (a very popular sound recording app among musicians).

While the future of writing apps may look different than the narrative I've written, consider that writing apps as we know them haven't changed much in forty years as I mentioned earlier. With emerging technology, writers will have such a need to evolve that it will be a no-brainer if someone offers them the ability to move to the cutting edge of technology and writing.

ESTIMATED TIME OF FUTURE ARRIVAL

I read a great book on futurism called *The Signals Are Talking: Why Today's Fringe is Tomorrow's Mainstream* by Amy Webb. It's a great book that explains how a futurist thinks about problems.

One of the questions she addresses is "How do I know when a certain future will arrive?"

She explains the power of thinking about the future like a GPS.

Your GPS tells you your estimated time of arrival at your destination, but your ETA can change. You might hit a traffic jam, an accident, make a wrong turn, or even encounter better traffic than usual. Your GPS constantly recalculates your ETA.

Looking at future technology and trends, it's helpful to think of them in this way too.

For example, if we agree that AI audiobook narration will become mainstream at some point, what factors might accelerate its ETA, and what factors might slow its arrival?

Webb talks about the distinction between express lanes and roadblocks.

Let me give you what I think is a very timely example right

now that will probably become dated in a few years. You will at first wonder why I am mentioning this, but trust me.

At the time of this writing, Tik Tok is one of the fastest-growing social media apps in the world. Users love the ability to make short and entertaining videos, usually with fun music choices.

Tik Tok's parent company, ByteDance, is headquartered in China. During the 2020 election cycle in the United States, there were national security concerns that the Chinese government was using Tik Tok to potentially spy on Americans and influence the election. The concerns may or may not have been valid, but US federal and state officials began posturing and threatening to ban Tik Tok from the United States. Companies such as Amazon made true on the threat, banning the app from its company phones. ByteDance maintained that there was no communication with the Chinese government and that Tik Tok was established in the United States, outside of the Chinese government's purview.

Right around this same time in the summer of 2020, Byte-Dance also released a new mobile phone app called Tomato Smooth Listening (Fanqie Changting). Don't let the name distract you; it is an audiobook listening app that allows readers to listen to audiobooks narrated not by humans, but by AI. Yes, that's right—an audiobook app where AI narrators read the books, not humans.

When it comes to the future of artificial intelligence, it's hard not to see the biggest advancements coming out of China. They're far more technologically advanced than the rest of the world, as it has been a key focus of the Chinese government. When it comes to voice AI, the Chinese language is easier to program with natural language processing than English, for example.

If the United States were to ban Tik Tok, either for a short period of time or indefinitely, that would introduce a roadblock to the progress of AI audiobook narration *for the United States*, particularly if ByteDance's app were successful and caught on internationally.

More than likely, the app is a small step toward AI narration and not the watershed moment.

What else would have to be true in order for the future to arrive?

For starters, audiobook services would have to allow AI narration. Today, none of them do. Audible in particular explicitly states in its terms that audiobooks must be read by a human.

Is it possible that a competitor will spring up solely for AI narration? That's unlikely. What's more plausible is that Audible and the other audiobook retailers are already planning for this future. It wouldn't surprise me if they released their own voice library that users could choose from. They've already done this with Alexa, offering a Samuel L. Jackson voice. Or, they may offer the opportunity for existing narrators with a certain number of audiobook finished hours (say, 100) to transform their voices into a persona. Their persona would read a cheaper version of the audiobook that would appear next to the traditionally-narrated one.

There are many roadblocks that would have to be removed for AI narration to move into the figurative express lane so that it can reach us. But thinking about it in terms of an ETA is useful.

COMPLIANCE

There are certain things in the writing life that aren't writing, marketing, or business, yet we have to do them.

General Data Protection Regulation (GDPR) in the European Union is an example.

Adhering to GDPR isn't going to sell you any books, but it'll help you avoid legal trouble.

I call this area of the writing life "compliance." You must learn compliance to play nice and be a good industry citizen.

My law degree is a specialization of risk management and compliance. I deal with it every day in my insurance career.

The longer I am an author, the more I realize the importance of anticipating and responding to compliance items. Let me give you a few examples.

I received an email from YouTube advising that certain integrations with their application programming interface (API) would soon stop working. An API is like a plug-socket arrangement where developers can plug into a company's servers to download data. The developer agrees to abide by the company's protocols in exchange for the data. I used a WordPress plugin that used the YouTube API to display all my videos in a grid on my website so that first-time visitors could watch my channel, subscribe, and like my videos without having to leave my website. If the API didn't work, I'd have to find another solution. I had to figure out first if the announcement applied to me, and if it did, how to rectify the situation. If I did nothing and it affected me, I risked having a broken page on my site and therefore a poor visitor experience. That's how compliance works. You have to spend time, money, and effort to stay compliant or there are consequences.

That same week, I also received a notification that there had been a security breach at a website that I frequent. My password was reset out of abundance of caution. I had to sign in, change my password, verify that nothing unusual happened with my account, and then change my passwords at other websites that used the same breached password. If I didn't do that, I risked being hacked.

The next week, I discovered that my Amazon affiliate links on YouTube were not compliant with the Amazon Associates terms of service in light of new Federal Trade Commission changes that had taken effect in the United States over the past year. I had to amend my affiliate disclosure on all videos on my channel. Fortunately, I found a tool that could do it in a few minutes, but it cost me $20.

Compliance won't sell books, but if you don't keep up with the industry, you will almost certainly *lose* book sales. It's perhaps more useful to think about compliance as a way to keep your money.

A big lesson for me this year was to allocate a budget for compliance, even if it's small. A *lot* of little compliance issues hit my inbox this year—more than usual. At one point in the second quarter, I was receiving compliance-related emails every week. I had to stop what I was doing to investigate and rectify the issues.

That is one of the downsides to being a long-term indie.

Sometimes it feels like I'm playing a tennis match with the world to keep my books for sale. Little things can force my books out of print or cut off my revenue streams if I'm not vigilant.

Let me give you another example of how not staying vigilant will cost you. I used a site called Kit to showcase the gear I use for my YouTube videos. It allows you to use Amazon Associates affiliate links. Kit was acquired by Patreon, but Patreon couldn't acquire the domain Kit.com, so then they sold it to Genius Link. It's a long story...

Instead, Genius Link had to change the domain name to Kit.co, which rendered all of the Kit.com links invalid.

I knew about the domain issue and I followed the instructions that Kit recommended to convert my links. However, I missed the news that Kit got acquired *again*, and the instructions changed, so my links didn't get converted. I didn't find out about this until a year later, when all of my links were beyond broken. I lost a lot of affiliate income, more than I care to share with you. (I should also mention that I didn't have my sales report tool when this happened, so I didn't even know that the revenue stream was choked off. I just thought people were buying less affiliate items...That's how compliance wounds you. Sometimes you don't know you have a problem until it's too late.)

Hopefully, you will learn from my experience that compliance is important.

Moving forward, I've decided to allocate a couple hundred dollars annually for compliance-related expenses. It might include buying tools, consulting with an attorney specifically for an industry legal issue, or the cost to pay a developer to fix something on my various websites. If I don't use the money, it's a win, but if I need it, I'll have allocated money for it.

YOUR BRAND IS EVERYTHING

In July 2020, the self-publishing community was rocked by a report that Mark Dawson *bought 400 copies of his book to secure a top 10 spot on the Sunday* Times *bestseller list.*

The first instinct of most in the community was to comment on the ethics of what Dawson did and to weigh in on whether they supported or decried his behavior.

I like Mark. It's undeniable that he's made our community a better place. I certainly have learned a few things from him. After reviewing the practices of bulk buying, I can understand *why* he thought what he did was okay. I still think it was wrong —not illegal, but borderline unethical. I think Mark misjudged the consequences and optics of his decision—but we all do that from time to time.

But when the story broke, I paid more attention to how the community responded. I noticed three things in particular.

First, cancel culture is a continued problem in our community. If anyone makes one false step, they get canceled. Gone are the days of forgiveness and grace.

Everyone makes mistakes. Everyone. Some mistakes are worse than others.

I've been around long enough to remember another author by the name of John Locke, a bestselling author who earned his success (in part) by *buying fake reviews and engaging in other unethical behavior*. Dawson is no John Locke. Not by a long shot.

I believe people can and do change if they are forgiven and provided a chance to prove they can do better. Not everyone improves, but *everyone* should be given the chance to do so. No exceptions.

We've lost our ability to forgive as a society, and that trend continues to be true in the indie community.

Whatever you believe about Dawson's actions, they don't warrant being canceled, but a lot of people have done that to him.

Second, Dawson's behavior forced a number of organizations, podcast hosts, and websites affiliated with him to take a stance on the matter. Their discomfort in commenting on the matter was palpable. Dawson's actions affected the entire community by virtue of his influence. And Dawson's influence cannot be understated—he had achieved bestseller status, a vibrant community around his marketing philosophies, a popular podcast, an amazingly successful course platform, and deep connections to the key players in the indie community.

This was not the case with John Locke—everyone lined up against him.

Third, Dawson's behavior after the event broke left questions about whether he made the situation worse. I'm not going to comment on this because, again, I don't think it's important for the sake of this book.

I learned three things from this event.

First, everyone makes mistakes. It's important to have a contingency plan for when *you* do. If you think you're immune to cancel culture, cancel culture will come for you one day.

Also, this is another reason not to participate in cancel culture. It's cancer, and karma's a bitch. I've been saying this for years, and I'll keep saying it. This story only proves my point.

Second, if you're an influencer or have any kind of platform, you need a contingency plan on what to do when *someone connected to you* makes an ethical misstep like this. The community will look to you for a stance, and for guidance. Your contingency plan needs to include a statement that clearly defines where you stand and denounces bad behavior, written in a professional and short manner. Your plan should also include how you will sever ties with the person or company if the situation warrants it. Not all situations do. Sometimes there's money at stake and you have to make tough choices. When these things happen, you have to do *something* because you'll lose credibility if you don't. The other person will drag your brand down with theirs.

Third, a public relations plan would have helped Mark considerably. A simple, honest apology with a promise to do better never goes out of style. A plan for how to communicate with his audience and online course communities would have also spared him some of the wrath the community unleashed on him.

In 2018, Chris Syme wrote an obscure little book called *Crisis Management for Authors*. It's a short book on how to navigate online crises and protect your reputation as an author.

I bought the book shortly after launch, mainly to support her for writing a book like this that so many people would ignore. She clearly had this book on her heart. At the time of this writing, the book has seven reviews and an Amazon sales rank of 750,000, which means it's not selling well.

Now, all of a sudden, it's the most relevant book any author can buy. It still probably won't become a bestseller, but if you have the ears to hear its message, you'll be better off than most.

What makes this situation so difficult is that Dawson is not a shady, spammy nonfiction author trying to make a dollar off the backs of innocent authors. He is a skilled fiction author, marketer, and businessperson. His courses taught a generation of authors how to make profitable Facebook ads. There are writers who owe their full-time living to Mark Dawson and the skills he taught them.

This is a gentle reminder that no matter who you are, your brand is everything. It takes years to build it, and seconds to destroy it.

Anyway, I have updated my contingency plan accordingly.

SAY YES EVEN WHEN IT HURTS

In the Technology section when discussing my personalized rules engine, I went on a tangent about saying yes to opportunities and following your gut.

To call this a learning about becoming a writer of the future is a stretch, but my programming adventures got me thinking about a few times in my life where the course of my entire life changed because I said yes to something that seemed innocent at the time but became very, very important.

My high school had a community service requirement in order to graduate. As a teenager, I would have rather played video games or read books, but my mom found me an opportunity to volunteer with the American Red Cross YouthCorps. I had a bunch of opportunities I could have pursued, but I chose the Red Cross because the work seemed more important.

I remember showing up to the Red Cross headquarters on a rainy afternoon after school. I had no idea what to expect. I ended up stuffing envelopes for an hour, but I got along with the volunteer director, so I enjoyed chatting with her every week. The next week, another group of teenagers attended, and we stuffed envelopes together. We became great friends, and I ended up bringing some more of my friends in band to volunteer every Friday. One of those people was a quirky guy I'd just met who played saxophone with me in band—on those Friday-afternoon drives, we bonded and became best friends. We wrote music together, and that was the beginning of my songwriting stint. We'd volunteer at Red Cross, eat dinner at the Outback Steakhouse, and then go to my grandmother's basement and write music until midnight.

I logged 365 hours of volunteer work with the Red Cross over four years. I volunteered there so much that I ran into the CEO numerous times in the cafeteria. We hit it off, and because I represented the youth groups so well and because I could talk business (at the ripe old age of seventeen!), he invited me to formally join the Board of Directors of my local American Red Cross. Yes, you read that correctly. At seventeen years old, I sat in board meetings with millionaires, and I had voting rights. I gained a lot of business acumen by sitting in those meetings and being a keen observer of human behavior. Honestly, I learned more from seeing the nervous heads of department get grilled by difficult questions than I did anything else. I learned how to ask difficult questions and get to the heart of issues quickly, mostly by mimicking other board members. I carried this skill with me as I grew older. Being able to sniff out issues and real problems despite tons of background noise is one of my key skills; it served me well in corporate America, in law school, and in my writing life.

Anyway, I've gone down a long tangent to show that sometimes decisions that seem inconsequential can make a big difference in your life.

In college, I majored in English and Spanish. When I graduated, I wanted to be a writer. I assumed that I would never use my Spanish degree. I loved speaking the language, and traveling abroad to Costa Rica, Nicaragua, and Panama was one of my college highlights, but I wasn't fluent, and I didn't see how I would ever achieve fluency.

My first job out of college was as a claims adjuster. It was my job to determine who was at fault for car accidents. It was a brutal and exhausting job. The first week of the job, the associate director came to my desk and asked me to join him in a conference room. I thought I was going to get fired. He had a copy of my resume, and said that he noticed I spoke Spanish. He was starting a bilingual claims unit and he couldn't find anyone who was qualified to do the job. He asked if I was interested, and told me he'd give me a seven percent pay differential if I said yes.

Keep in mind that I wasn't fluent in Spanish at this point. I spoke Spanish like Tarzan, and my skill level was laughable at best. But I said yes on the spot.

I barely spoke Spanish, but now I had to become *fluent* in it. The first six weeks were really, really hard. Customers couldn't understand me, and I couldn't understand them. I was speaking Spanish all day, so much that my English was starting to suffer. True story.

Around six months, something clicked. Suddenly, I understood everything, and customers understood me. I was switching between English and Spanish without thinking. Customers were calling my boss to tell him how much they appreciated me. One customer told me, "Señor, you speak some strange Spanish, but I understand you, and I appreciate you helping me and my family in our difficult time."

I did so well in that job that I was promoted quickly, into progressively better jobs that now give me the flexibility to write. Learning how to become fluent in Spanish is one of the reasons I am able to learn quickly, particularly programming languages—which leads me to the personalized rules engine and having to learn Python.

All because I said yes to an opportunity that seemed insurmountable at the time.

My writing life is filled with decisions that seemed unimportant at the time: starting a YouTube channel, writing a book that mixed my philosophies on writing with coping with being abandoned by my biological father, and randomly pitching a speech idea to a conference organizer that got me in front of a crowd of 1,000 people...with a pitch that I pulled out of the air.

Anyway, I'm not suggesting to say yes to everything. That's never a good idea. But sometimes big opportunities come disguised as trivial decisions. One of the reasons I've been so successful in life is because I've opened myself to opportunities and connections that didn't seem important or that suit my "agenda" at the time.

You never know where life will lead you.

A SWOT ANALYSIS OF THE INDIE AUTHOR PROFESSION

What does the writer of the future look like, and what challenges do they face?

A few things have been clear to me for a few years.

First, Amazon, while committed to its KDP program, is not committed to *innovating* the platform. As of July 2020, the KDP dashboard hasn't changed much since the program's inception aside from some cosmetic changes and a couple of feature updates. The upload process and the amount of relative data you have access to have not changed. The same is generally true with the other book retailers.

Second, it's difficult for entrepreneurs to create products for writers. Indie authors are price-sensitive, and rightfully so given the amount of money they have to invest into their books. If a product doesn't fall within the two "sweet spots" of writing and marketing, it will die in our community. Indies will not buy it because they are so focused on writing and selling books. There are rare exceptions, such as Book Funnel and Vellum, but authors only pay for those because formatting and book delivery are such a pain in the ass that they're willing to do something about it. There are other pains in the ass that they're willing to live with, however, such as calculating their book sales.

The lack of innovation and entrepreneurial investment in the indie space means that indie authors are going to be in a lot of trouble in a few years. Our progress as a community is dependent on the breadcrumbs retailers give us, and our financial prudence disincentivizes people from starting new products and services outside of the usual sweet spots for fear of losing money. This is why I believe that so many indies search elsewhere for solutions to the problems they have, such as the platforms of digital marketers and other entrepreneurs whose advice is not always a good fit for what we do.

Traditional publishers haven't gotten around to adopting emerging technology yet, but I'll bet good money that the coronavirus pandemic has them reevaluating their business model. If they haven't started looking into automation and artificial intelligence as a way to sell more books, they will. Before COVID-19, there was no incentive for them to change their business models. Now, they can't afford NOT to.

It will take years for traditional publishers to get the technology right, but it'll happen. And when it does, do you think indies will be able to compete with them by doing the same things they're doing today? The cutting edge scrappiness that we've had for the last decade will become irrelevant.

Combine that with new generations of more tech-savvy writers, new generations of writers from developing countries who to date have never had a voice but will through the power of AI translation, cultural preferences in emerging superpowers such as China that may place less emphasis on western books, and an ever-shifting sociopolitical landscape...and you have a recipe for mass indie author extinction. Our world of publishing is going to look very different in 2030 and 2035.

My fear is that as emerging technology becomes prominent, it will be inapplicable or unaffordable for indies, such as artificial intelligence. If we can't adopt emerging tech, we'll be left behind. We'll find ourselves in the exact same position that traditional publishers were a decade ago—decrying new technology and romanticizing the way we do business.

That's why I believe that we have to start finding ways to adopt emerging technology *ourselves*, *right now*, because no one else is going to do it for us. Writing books and marketing those books is important, but we have to be careful not to focus on those tasks so much that the rest of the world passes us by.

If you want to innovate your business, you'll have to fight to make it happen, and you'll be alone.

And yes, that might mean learning an entirely new skill, such as the basics of a programming language. Or hiring someone to do it for you.

Like I said, don't expect book retailers or entrepreneurs to do it for you. Any change we get will likely be incremental, and the tools we get may not be the tools we truly need.

If you refuse to adapt and innovate, you will be left behind.

I recognize that I may sound alarmist. I hope I'm wrong. But history and human nature are good teachers. All industries become stagnant at some point, usually because of bad choices, lack of foresight, and the inability to accept change. Today's innovators are tomorrow's resistors. If you need examples, look no further than the American car manufacturing industry, the retail industry (what's left of it), and the cell phone industry prior to the advent of the iPhone. And of course, traditional publishers—but you knew I was going to say that.

There may very well be two writers of the future—those who adopt the skills and tech needed to compete in a new marketplace, and those who have to fight to survive because they didn't see the warning signs. The latter group will always be behind the curve, unable to catch up.

I choose to be in the first group.

IDEAS YOU CAN STEAL

THE NEUROSCIENCE OF WRITING
AND READING

The science of reading is fascinating. More fascinating is the science of writing!

What is it in our brains that compels us to pick up the pen or sit down at the keyboard? What happens to our brains when we write? What happens to readers' brains when they read?

I am sure that there are scientists whose life work is studying the science of reading and writing. What might we learn from their research?

It would be interesting if someone with a degree in neuroscience wrote a book about it. Lisa Cron wrote two great books on the topic, but there's so much more to be explored.

What about biohacking and writing? What kind of futures might be possible there?

Or the most cutting edge research around reading and writing, particularly with e-readers, smartphones, and tablets?

There's a lot in this arena that has yet to be explored.

AUTHOR SERVICING CO-OP

In the Marketing section, I talked about the difference between sales and servicing and how, long-term, you need a way to draw a clean line between sales and service in your writing business. For most successful writers, that means hiring an assistant.

However, most writers can't afford a virtual assistant. It's asinine to even suggest it.

What if a group of authors at a similar career level pooled their resources as a co-op into a single or set of virtual assistants who worked on all of their behalf?

The going rate for a competent virtual assistant these days is around $40/hour, minimum. The good assistants command more than that. For full-time work, that would cost around $1,600 per week, $6,400 per month, or $76,800 per year. Those numbers don't include benefits, of course, but this would be a freelancing relationship.

If ten authors formed a co-op, they could each pay $7,680 per year for access to a reader concierge service. That's around $160 per week or $640 per month. Is it expensive? Yes, but it's cheaper than $6,400 per month.

The authors would have to agree on what types of emails

the assistant would handle and which ones would be forwarded to the respective author. I could see a service like this being very good at answering questions like:

- "What's the best series to start with?"
- "Is this book in paperback, or at Kobo, or at my local bookstore?"
- "Do you have a Patreon page?"
- "Would you like to be on my podcast?"

You know, the common questions. Authors could also ask for dedicated help with a book launch, or for basic proofreading or website maintenance.

The co-op could be a white label service; each author would set up a dedicated email for the assistant and have their contact form routed to them. The assistant would work through the writers' inbox several times a day, answering the questions they can and deferring to the authors for any they can't. From the readers' perspective, it would look like the author has a full-time assistant. The assistant would have to have impeccable customer service skills, of course, and go above and beyond for the reader.

The author could log in to the assistant's email address at any time to see the emails that have been handled.

Honestly, this could be an author services company that, as it gains more authors, hires more assistants and offers access to a service that was previously inaccessible to most authors.

There are virtual assistant "companies" on the market, but they cater to a generic audience. I've used them in the past, and the big challenge is training them to understand how an author business works. The value in a service like this is that it would be specifically for writers.

YOUR SELF-PUBLISHING ATTORNEY

Years ago, I secured a trademark for one of my series. I could have hired a local law firm to research the mark and file the applications, but instead, I hired an attorney over the Internet who specialized in trademarks. More specifically, trademarks were the *only* thing he did.

What made him more unique was that he charged flat fees for every service needed. I knew exactly what I was getting for run-of-the-mill trademark work. While I don't necessarily believe he was cheaper than the traditional alternative, it sure felt like it. I also appreciated his transparency. His business is booming, and he's an expert in trademark law.

Why don't we have more attorneys in the publishing space that do this? I can only count the number of attorneys I know who assist self-published writers on one hand, and all of them charge hourly.

It would be interesting if there was an attorney or law firm that provided flat fee services to authors.

They'd charge X amount to send a cease and desist letter for copyright infringement, X for publishing contract reviews based on how many pages are in the contract, and X for wills and X per hour to answer legal questions. They'd help you with copyright permission questions.

The more successful you become, the more legal questions you have, especially around taxes and running a business. Having been to law school, my experience is that local law firms that don't specialize in authors are generally bad fits for these types of questions. For example, my family law attorney screwed me something awful with how we structured my estate because they didn't understand writing businesses and copyright. It was an expensive mistake to fix.

Since authors are cost-conscious, the prospect of calling a lawyer and hoping you can afford their fees usually puts most authors off. It would be far better to charge flat rates and publish those on a website.

A service like this could bring in a steady stream of customers and likely be a pretty good way to make a living.

YOUR SELF-PUBLISHING ACCOUNTANT

If a flat-fee attorney for self-publishers is a good idea, then so is an accountant!

Fortunately, accountants are more plentiful. Many offer flat fees, and there are many who specialize in digital entrepreneurs. I don't know of any who specialize in self-published writers, though. That doesn't mean they don't exist.

If someone wanted to jump into this space, here's the can't-fail blueprint for success: write *the* definitive book on taxes and bookkeeping for self-published writers. Expand your audience to creatives if that makes sense. Start a YouTube channel with a weekly tax tip in 5-10 minutes or less. Promote the hell out of yourself—it wouldn't be hard because you would be the only one...

Next, publish your fees on your site and drive traffic through Google AdSense, Facebook, and YouTube, and double your ad spend leading up to tax time. Market to authors but let people know you specialize in self-publishing. Get yourself on all the major podcasts and YouTube channels. Partner with Your Self-Publishing Attorney to offer special consulting packages. Then, wait for the leads to come in.

The hard part about finding an accountant in publishing is making sure you select someone who has experience with authors who have many streams of income. Just because someone is a certified accountant doesn't mean they know how to handle *your* taxes.

When I first started publishing, I used an accountant friend. My first year of publishing was simple. Then, every year, I called her with more difficult questions.

"Hey, I got twenty 1099s this year."

"Hey, I'm hiring a video editor. What do I need to do?"

"Hey, I just accepted a part-time job from a company based in London. Am I good?"

"Hey, I may sign a film deal this year. How would I potentially handle a large payment?"

"Hey, I'd like to form a trust. Oh, and I'd also like to incorporate my business. How do I protect my assets?"

She gave up on me because my operations were so different from her typical clients, which were local brick and mortar businesses whose tax complexity was much simpler.

That's why, just as it's a good idea to hire a book cover designer and editor who have experience in your genre, it's also a good idea to hire an accountant who understands the writing profession.

TRACK YOUR BOOK WRITING TIME

I gave a podcast interview where the interviewer asked me how I stopped outlining.

I described how, with my book *Android Paradox*, I timed how long it took me to do everything: outlining, rough draft, subsequent drafts, revising, formatting, and working with my editor and cover designer. I knew how long it took me to create the novel down to the minute.

I took the data and put it into a chart. Outlining took me the most time by far. I asked why. It was due to the research.

Then I asked how outlining affected my draft.

I realized that my finished novel deviated from the outline a lot. In fact, near the end, I broke away from my outline entirely.

Then I asked the breakthrough question: if I was spending all this time outlining only to ignore it, why was I outlining?

I made a commitment to reduce the amount of time I spent outlining with my next novel. Eventually, I stopped doing it.

As I told that story on the podcast, I reconnected with my earlier self, where I was just trying to figure everything out. In retrospect, that one little experiment that I did on a whim for curiosity's sake—timing my novel—resulted in one of the biggest successes in learning how to be prolific.

I didn't abandon outlining until I was ready.

I often ask writers to figure out where their time is going. Most people *think* they know, but they actually don't.

So that's my idea: time yourself as you write your next book and see what you learn.

VISUALIZE YOUR TOOLBOX

What's in your writer toolbox?

Aside from our computers, most of the tools we use in our business are virtual.

I believe that learning how to command your toolbox is important. I've collected a lot of tools over the years, and I'm good at knowing when a certain tool is appropriate for a task. I'm always asking, "What tools do I already have that can help me execute what I'm trying to accomplish?"

For fun, I created a mind map that laid out all the tools I currently use in my business. Maybe this will be helpful for me in the future, but if anything, it was a helpful refresher to understand what I have in my box so I can be intentional about using the right tool at the right time.

There's nothing worse than executing something like a marketing campaign and realizing that you had a tool that could have helped you do it better. For example, last year, I sent out advanced review copies for one of my books. It was a pain to follow up and chase reviews. I forgot that Book Funnel had a feature called "Certified Mail" that handles all the administration for you. You enter the email addresses of your reviewers, a welcome message, a follow-up reminder, and a final reminder when the book is live. Book Funnel's system handles the rest. I used the feature with the book launch for *150 Self-Publishing Questions Answered*, and it made everything much smoother.

To convey the concept of visualizing your toolbox, I used a tool called Mindomo to create a mind map that visualized my tools. You can view it at *www.authorlevelup.com/writertoolbox*.

KNOWLEDGE TRANSFER PLATFORM

Indie authors have careers because they turn their imagination into income.

Ideas equal income. So does knowledge.

There are so many people out there that have knowledge but don't do anything with it beyond their own personal gain. For example, if you're a nuclear scientist, you're unlikely to talk about nuclear science outside of your own circles; otherwise, you'll bore people.

But there is a writer out there that needs to know about nuclear science. In fact, maybe their book revolves around it, and they need to learn about nuanced details that they can't find on the Internet.

What if there was a platform that connected interested people like writers with people who have subject matter expertise?

Need an astrophysicist to review your space opera to check for implausible science? Need a police officer to verify if the police procedure you wrote is accurate? Need a carpenter to verify that your general contractor character is using the right terminology when they're building a house?

This platform would put you in contact with people who have the expertise you need.

Imagine posting a job that explains what you need, and then experts bidding to win the work. You can review their profiles to see which person would be the best fit. You send them what you need, pay their fee, maybe jump on a quick conference call. You walk away with a book that is 100% more realistic and the expert gets paid for it.

There would be experts for everything from nuclear science to sewing, and the people wouldn't necessarily be world-renowned. It might be a mom who sews on weekends but is really passionate about it because her grandmother taught her how to do it. She might be your greatest asset in writing your cozy mystery novel about a heroine who likes to sew.

One of the hardest parts about writing is writing what you don't know. There's only so much you can research before you need help. It's not exactly easy to ask random people a bunch of questions. Personally, I always feel self-conscious about this. It would be much easier if there was a platform that facilitated it.

THE INDIE AUTHOR APPRENTICE

I received an email from one of my YouTube subscribers; he was in high school and decided he wanted to be a writer. He was going to college in the fall and wanted to know what he could do every day to accomplish his dream. Not only did the email make me feel old, it got me thinking about the next generation of self-published writers and how they will establish their careers.

It's 2020 as I write this chapter. The next generation of self-published writers are probably in elementary and middle school right now, so when they come of age in 2030, they're going to be completely different than us.

For starters, they'll be more tech and data savvy. The tools and processes we use today may seem barbaric to them, but they'll have a strong desire to know what they don't know. They'll have the power of optimism, but we'll have the power of wisdom and experience (in ten years, I'll be 43...not sure I'll have much wisdom, but I'll certainly have experience).

How do we foster and support the next generation?

I believe the age-old apprentice system could be helpful. In that system, a "master" takes on an "apprentice," and the apprentice does much of the work under the master's supervision. After a few years, the apprentice knows enough to establish their own trade.

What would a master-apprentice setup look like in a digital world?

In ten to twenty years, self-publishing will be more viable and mainstream than it is today—with more people jumping into the industry, it's only a matter of time before more self-published authors become successful, igniting more awareness of it. I also think that college and MFA programs will continue to embrace self-publishing as a viable option, which means that future generations of young people will be exposed to it.

Imagine if a successful author who is making a living from their writing hires an apprentice. The apprentice is a fledgling but driven writer who wants to write books for a living. The apprenticeship would be a part-time job (unless the writer can afford to pay a full-time salary).

The apprentice serves the master author in every area of the business. They watch as the master brainstorms and plans a new book, they see the rough manuscript that the master produces, help with edits, coordinate formatting and cover design, assist the master with marketing, answer customer service emails, maintain the master's website, moderate the master's communities on places like Facebook, and other odd jobs that come up in the life of an indie author. Their role would serve the function of a general virtual assistant, and it would give them exposure to all areas of running an author business.

In exchange for the apprentice's time and effort, the master would also build in time for the apprentice to work on their own books, and the master would review and offer feedback. The master would also meet with the apprentice regularly for mentorship conversations.

The master would also grant the apprentice free use of

his/her tools as well any other members on the master's team, such as other virtual assistants. The master would show the apprentice the secret tools of the trade, such as the nuts and bolts on how to write spellbinding fiction, tax tips, and other items that the apprentice would never find elsewhere.

The master would use their status, privilege, and influence to help the apprentice begin their career on solid footing. The master might even allow the apprentice to publish books under the master's publishing company for a short period of time, with copyrights reverting back to the apprentice upon completion of the program.

The master would let his or her community know that they have an apprentice and make the apprentice highly visible in everything the master did. This way, the community would rally around the apprentice and support them when it's time for them to leave.

This method would give the apprentice a fast, paid exposure to every facet of the publishing business from someone they can trust. They would get hands-on experience from an author who's much further down the road, possibly the furthest down the road you can be. Imagine how much you would learn from Stephen King if he did a program like this, for example. Being able to pick his brain and sit with him behind closed doors would be immensely valuable for a hungry, ambitious writer.

The master would get part-time help at a cheaper rate and know that they're giving back to the community. Of course, the master would have to ensure that they pick the *right* apprentice, preferably an author in the genre they write, and someone who will follow through and get the most out of the relationship. Someone looking for a lazy way to start a career would not be a good fit for the program, and the master would have to be extremely selective and rigorous in searching for the right person.

If I am ever in a position to do it, this is precisely how I would mentor someone from the next generation. It would be better than a college education by far. If I become a bestselling author with a multi six or seven-figure income someday, give me one to two years with an apprentice, and I would love to see what we could do.

WRITE ABOUT YOUR CAREER
EXPERIENCE

I believe that everyone has a writer's guide in them.

Writers always find themselves in situations where they need subject matter expertise. Maybe they need to put a firefighter on the page, but they don't know any firefighters.

What's the first thing a normal person would do if they wanted to learn about firefighting? They'd talk to a firefighter, of course. Or they'd do an Internet search and hope for the best.

But we writers are introverts. We'd much rather find a book about firefighting, preferably for authors by an author. A book titled *Into the Fire: The Writer's Guide to Getting Fire and Firefighters Right* would be the perfect book for them.

Is there a mass market potential? God no, but you could probably recoup your editing and cover costs, especially if you hire a cheap cover designer.

A book like this would be a lot easier to write than a novel, so you could write it quickly because you already know what needs to be written. A short 20,000- to 30,000-word book on the topic that teaches writers everything they need to know to write the subject matter realistically is underrated in my opinion.

A few years ago, I bought a writer's guide to the United States armed forces. It was very helpful as I wrote my space opera series *Galaxy Mavericks*.

I argue that there aren't enough subject matter books for writers on the market.

Even if you think your career so far is trivial, what's obvious to you is not obvious to a writer who wants to make their book better.

For example, one day, I plan to write a book on the insurance industry for writers. It's the least sexy book I can think of, but a writer somewhere, sometime is going to need to know how insurance companies operate and what the life of a claims adjuster or an insurance executive might look like. They'll need to get the details right. My book will be there for them.

Anyway, I'm not promising gold. I'm merely suggesting that you can cash in on your work experience, even if you hate your job. It'll do someone a lot of good.

LET'S HIRE A FUTURIST

I've been reading books by quantitative futurists this quarter. I'm interested in knowing how they think.

Did you know that companies hire futurists to help them project the future? For example, Royal Dutch Shell did this and incorporated futurism into its way of thinking. It helped them make record profit and avoid pitfalls that ensnared its competitors.

Wouldn't it be interesting if self-publishers as a community banded together and hired a futurist to review the publishing industry and trends outside the industry? The futurist could provide a report with scenarios of what the future of the self-published author would look like, with recommendations of what we need to start preparing for now.

Futurists have such a unique take on the world. They're not always right, but when they are, it's fascinating.

There are so many trends in the world right now that it's hard to know how they will converge and affect us. A futurist studies trends every day. They're more comfortable looking at them. Therefore, hiring one could be fruitful and productive for the industry.

Of course, this would probably be very expensive, but maybe someone could do a Kickstarter. Maybe it wouldn't be that hard for a futurist since we're such a small segment of the industry.

But in any case, tapping in to the mind of someone who has a good grip on the future could be very advantageous for self-published writers and help us stay nimble.

AUTHOR EFFICIENCY COACH

I don't hold myself out as a coach or a guru. I despise both of those words. Coaches and gurus think they have all the answers.

I don't. I'm still learning on my journey.

I've always rejected the idea of providing coaching services. It's lucrative, but I'm not the coaching type. I've taken on a handful of clients in the past couple years, but they approached me, and I only took on clients who were extremely driven. I don't offer my services to the public.

An idea I had, though, was coaching in an area that I'm good at—efficiency.

Michael La Ronn, Author Efficiency Coach? Doesn't have a good ring. But it's interesting. Call me up and let's talk about how efficient you are in your writing business—what tools do you use, what are your processes, and so on. It's an area that I'm uniquely qualified to coach.

But still, it doesn't get me excited. Someone else can steal it.

AUTHOR INSPIRATION, THE ALBUM?

I was reading an article about vinyl and how its comeback surprised everyone. Fifteen years ago, people couldn't give their records away fast enough. I used to go to record stores and I'd buy old vinyls for pennies on the dollar. Usually, the vinyl section would be in some dusty old room in the back that no one dared to explore.

Today, artists are releasing their albums in vinyl, and the vinyls are more expensive than CDs! The same albums I bought in the back room of a record store are worth quadruple what I paid for them fifteen years ago.

In a parenthetical aside in the article, the author asked an ill-informed question about why audiobooks aren't available in vinyl format.

Seriously?

Unless you want to buy a set of twenty vinyls, and you want to listen to audiobooks on a turntable, it's a bad idea.

That got me thinking what people *would* listen to on vinyl in the writing space. I remember listening to old comedy albums my dad and uncle used to collect. Richard Pryor, Bill Cosby, Pigmeat Markham...really good stuff, and perfect for listening in the background while you're making dinner, fixing up things around the house, etc. My great-grandfather used to play vinyls as background noise while he did projects around the house.

Anyway. Wouldn't it be cool if there was an album that consisted of successful writers giving their best writing advice in 5-7 minute-long tracks? Each author would tell their story in a personal way, like a storyteller at a festival. Each track would be like a piece of art, with a storyline, music, and maybe even sound effects—kind of like the first few episodes of my podcast, *The Writer's Journey*. The tone would be relaxed, slightly comical, and fun. That's the kind of content that would be perfect for a vinyl album. Almost like an audio documentary.

Actually, it would be perfect as an audiobook too.

CONTENT CREATED WHILE
WRITING THIS BOOK

150 Self-Publishing Questions Answered (Book)

This book was written in a partnership between Michael and The Alliance of Independent Authors (ALLi, a nonprofit organization for self-published writers), and it answers the most common self-publishing questions in a conversational question and answer format. The audiobook is narrated by Michael!

Buy your copy at www.authorlevelup.com/150

Author Level Up YouTube Channel - Highlights

Watch at youtube.com/authorlevelup.

The Ultimate Guide to Self-Publishing vs. Traditional Publishing - 2020

. . .

Copyright for Authors (playlist)

Interviews & Appearances

Draft2Digital Live with Michael La Ronn: Michael sits down with D2D's director of marketing Kevin Tumlinson to talk about writing, life and productivity.

Remaining Relevant with Michael La Ronn (The Fearless Storyteller Podcast): With host Ethan Freckleton, Michael talks writing fiction, writer's block, and beating self-doubt so you can develop staying power with your author career.

Mental Models for Writers with Michael La Ronn (Twitter Chat): In this Twitter chat for the Alliance of Independent Authors, Michael talks about the power of mental models and how you can utilize them to advance your writing career.

READ THE NEXT VOLUME

Michael's writer journey continues in the next volume of this series!

Grab your copy at www.authorlevelup.com/confidential.

MEET M.L. RONN

Science fiction and fantasy on the wild side!

M.L. Ronn (Michael La Ronn) is the author of many science fiction and fantasy novels including *The Good Necromancer, Android X,* and *The Last Dragon Lord* series.

In 2012, a life-threatening illness made him realize that storytelling was his #1 passion. He's devoted his life to writing ever since, making up whatever story makes him fall out of his chair laughing the hardest. Every day.

Learn more about Michael
www.authorlevelup.com (for writers)
www.michaellaronn.com (fiction)

MORE BOOKS BY M.L. RONN

More Books for Writers:

www.authorlevelup.com/books

Fiction:
www.michaellaronn.com/books